D1221287

6: PERSPECTIVES IN CRITICISM

PERSPECTIVES IN CRITICISM

6:

Helen Caldwell

The Brazilian Othello
of Machado de Assis

A STUDY OF DOM CASMURRO

UNIVERSITY OF CALIFORNIA PRESS
Berkeley and Los Angeles
1960

PENNSYLVANIA MILITARY COLLEGE
CHESTER, PENNSYLVANIA
LIBRARY
47829

DISCARDED UNIVERSITY COPY

PQ9677
.M18D69

© 1960 by The Regents of the University of California

University of California Press
Berkeley and Los Angeles, California
Cambridge University Press
London, England

LIBRARY OF CONGRESS CATALOG CARD NO. 60-6518
Printed in the United States of America
Designed by Ward Ritchie

Preface

THE BRAZILIANS have a jewel for all the world to envy, a veritable Kohinoor among writers of fiction—Machado de Assis. But, more than any other people, we of the English-speaking world should envy Brazil this writer who so constantly used our Shakespeare as his model—so neatly fused into his own stories the characters, plots, and ideas of Shakespeare—that we may flatter ourselves that only we can truly appreciate the great Brazilian.

We find encouragement for this megalomania in the attitude of Brazilian writers, who are wont to refer to Machado de Assis as their "enigma," their "myth," their "Sphinx."[1] Baffled by his subtlety, many of them have turned to his life, have tried to interpret his writings in terms of his humble origin and physical make-up.[2] But Machado de Assis deliberately withheld the facts of his private life, because apparently he felt such facts had little to do with his life of the spirit and that a knowledge of them would only hinder appreciation of his works.[3] He frequently tells us in effect: my writings are my life, by my works ye shall know me.[4] And he cautions us to read carefully[5]—for pattern and purpose are so artfully integrated in each of his writings that every part, however seemingly disconnected, goes to form the meaning of the whole.

In the following study I have tried to obey these

47829

two injunctions of the author. Since the collected writings of Machado de Assis present the steady, consistent emergence of an intellect, with ideas and forms occurring, recurring, developing, I have drawn on his other works for elucidation of a single novel. Since Machado himself referred many of his recurring ideas to Shakespeare, I have tried to trace such (pertinent) references to their source. But the core of my study consists in answering two questions that rise directly out of *Dom Casmurro* itself—one subsidiary to the other. The main question is "Was the heroine guilty of adultery?"; the subsidiary one, "Why was the novel so written that it seems to leave the question of the heroine's guilt or innocence to the decision of the reader?"

Although *Dom Casmurro* was published in 1900, no comprehensive analysis of it has yet appeared. Those students of Machado de Assis who have mentioned this novel have, almost without exception, assumed the guilt of its heroine;[6] but there is little indication that any real study has been given the matter.

The second question has not even been formulated by writers on Machado de Assis, yet an answer to *it* would seem to be an essential part of the answer to the main question, if not the key to it.

The evidence I have marshaled for answering these two questions will, I hope, shed light on Machado de Assis's message in this novel and in his others, and furnish some small insight into his narrative method.

It is a pleasant duty to thank the friends who have cheered this little book on its way with their help and encouragement.

On the campus of the University of California, Los Angeles, there are Ada Nisbet and John J. Espey of the English department; Albert H. Travis, chairman of Classics, and Paul Friedlander of the same department; and there is Marion A. Zeitlin, formerly my teacher, still my kindly bulwark and mentor in things Brazilian —to all these goes my sincere gratitude.

I wish to thank the Brazilian Ministry of Foreign Affairs for placing at my disposal a microfilm of the manuscript of *Esaú e Jacob* and for the sympathetic support given me at all times through its consulate in Los Angeles: I am most deeply indebted to former consuls Sérgio Corrêa da Costa, Antonio Corrêa do Lago, and Galba Samuel Santos, and to the present consul, Raul de Smandek, a friend of long standing.

My heartfelt thanks are here expressed to Ilda Stichini, who has shared with me her insight into Portuguese literature.

Thanks are due the library staff of the University of California, Los Angeles—in particular to members of the reference department, and to my fellow Portuguese student Helene Schimansky of the catalog department.

A special word of appreciation goes to John H. Jennings and James Kubeck of the University of California Press for their solicitous concern over this book and for their gentle patience with its author.

Acknowledgment is made to the Noonday Press for permission to quote from my translation of *Dom Casmurro* (1953).

HELEN CALDWELL

Contents

1

Santiago's Love Story

MACHADO DE ASSIS's first novel appeared in 1872. Twenty-eight years later he published his masterpiece, *Dom Casmurro*—perhaps the finest of all American novels of either continent.[1] In both books, the reader witnesses the struggle of love and jealousy for possession of a man's heart, with love going down to tardy but complete defeat.

Jealousy never ceased to fascinate Machado de Assis. Throughout his works, in articles as well as fiction, he often paused to stick a leisurely scalpel into some new manifestation of jealousy. Jealousy has a fat part in seven of his nine novels; the plots of ten short stories[2] turn upon the ugly passion—though in seven of the latter, to be sure, it receives an ironic if not rudely comic treatment.

Shakespeare's *Othello* is brought into the argument of twenty-eight stories, plays, and articles.[3] *Othello* is not the only play of Shakespeare's that Machado de Assis hitched to his starry wagon. *Romeo and Juliet* serves as a plot for one novel and two short pieces. The character of Hamlet has a way of creeping in—even into his Othelloes. Ophelia, Jaques, Caliban, Lady Macbeth, and others turn up miraculously in the suburbs of Rio de Janeiro. But let us stay for the present with *Othello* and *Dom Casmurro*.

Machado de Assis turned over the narration of *Dom*

Casmurro to a figment of his imagination—its hero Bento Santiago, a fifty-seven-year-old recluse living in a suburb of Rio de Janeiro. Santiago calls himself an "Othello," but his disengaging air of frankness, calm impartiality, and reasonableness more nearly resembles the bluff style of "honest Iago" than that of the impassioned Othello.

It is immediately apparent that this was a subtle man, and a lawyer into the bargain, whose words the reader will do well to weigh carefully. For example, in his first chapter he explains the title of his narrative: "Dom Casmurro" was a nickname conferred upon him by an irate neighbor and gleefully taken up by the whole neighborhood.

> Don't consult your dictionaries. *Casmurro* is not used here in the meaning they give for it, but in the sense in which the man in the street uses it, of a morose, tight-lipped man withdrawn within himself.[4]

But what if we consult our dictionaries? The definition he did not want us to see is this: "an obstinate, moodily stubborn, *wrong-headed* man." Perhaps we will decide that this older, standard definition fits Santiago better than the one *he* offers.[5]

First, however, let us run over the story of his love and jealousy as he set it down, without much questioning either his veracity or his ability to see things as they actually were.

It is he who discloses that his story is that of Othello, but with a certain important difference—his Desdemona was guilty. There are other less important differences. Our Brazilian Othello, at the beginning of his tale, was not a man of mature years, a proud dusky warrior in strange, rich dress, who had seen men with their heads growing beneath their shoulders. He was a fifteen-year-old boy given to daydreams that perhaps equaled in color and vividness the marvels the Moorish Othello knew. There was nothing hard and warlike

2

about Santiago—he was even somewhat cowardly: witness the position in which we first find him, hiding behind a door. He was Christian and Catholic, with an aversion to bloodshed, the only child of a wealthy widow, and tied to his mother's apron strings.

His Desdemona was the girl next door, Capitolina, or Capitú for short, only fourteen[6] but tall and well developed for her age—in fact she was a little taller than her hero. She was not a high-born Venetian, but a rather poor girl: her dress calico, her hands washed in well water and common soap, her shoes worn, and mended by herself; and, though like the other Desdemona she gazed upon her beauty in a mirror (presumably of Italian manufacture), it was a cheap little mirror bought for fifteen cents from an Italian peddler. Her father, Padua, like Brabantio, was connected with a branch of the government consulted in time of war (but of course Brazil was decidedly poverty-stricken in the matter of wars); he was not "a senator," only a poorly paid employee in the war department. He was an affectionate and good-natured man, but rather weak in the head, who turned over his salary and the other practical matters of life to his capable wife and beautiful, sensible daughter, so that he could spend all his serious thoughts on the building of cages for the canaries and tanagers of which he was an avid collector. It is even intimated that he was self-seeking, coarse and vulgar, and given to low company. But Capitú had the dignity and the pride of a high-born lady, and an understanding of life, men, and women, far beyond her years—far beyond that of the Venetian Desdemona.

Our Michael Cassio was Santiago's classmate Ezekiel Escobar. Like Cassio, Escobar was a great "mathematician," handsome, courteous, ingratiating. Like Cassio, he had a hand in Santiago's wooing, urged on the love affair between the young lovers, and acted as go-between for their letters.

The Iago of the story, according to our hero, was

3

José Dias, a trusted dependent of the Santiago household. Like his Shakespearean prototype, he devoted his energies to giving freely of his advice: he had no other regular occupation. Santiago said that he did it "just to make trouble," and this was the opinion of Cousin Justina, a poor relative who acted as companion to Santiago's mother.

When we first come upon the young Santiago he is eavesdropping outside the living room. Inside the room José Dias was reminding Bento's mother, Dona Gloria, that if she still intended Bento to be a priest it was time to go ahead and send him to the seminary; otherwise a serious obstacle might arise, if it had not already arisen. Pressed for an explanation, José Dias, with apparent reluctance, explained that Bento and Capitú were always "off together in corners," and if they should start making love she would have a problem on her hands. Dona Gloria exclaimed against this idea —they were only children and old playmates—but agreed that it was time to send Bento to the seminary.

It took but little reflection on Bento's part to recognize the truth of José Dias's words, that he *was* in love with Capitú and she with him. He went next door to find her carving their two names together on the garden wall.

The part about being a priest was an old story. Dona Gloria's first child had been born dead. She promised God that if He would send her a second child and it should be a boy she would make him a priest. In the past few years, however, nothing had been said about it, and Bento supposed the matter forgotten.

When Santiago told Capitú of his mother's decision to send him off to the seminary, Capitú was at first filled with anger and despair—anger against Dona Gloria—but finally looked at the problem practically and intelligently. After considering who might help them, she decided upon José Dias: he was clever and persuasive, he was fond of Bento and bound to work

4

for him as his future master. Bento should flatter him, convince him that he could not become a priest, and get him to work on Dona Gloria. Capitú was even willing to be separated from Bento for a time, so that he could go to São Paulo to study law, or even to Europe. José Dias liked to travel: he would be the one to accompany Bento, and if he wanted to go badly enough he would persuade Dona Gloria.

Santiago would have taken an easier way out: praying to God to change his mother's mind, getting the emperor (God's representative on earth) to interfere in favor of sending him to the medical school in Rio de Janeiro so that he would not have to leave the city and Capitú. Capitú rejected such chimerical schemes. Santiago followed her directions and won over José Dias by holding out the hope of the European trip. He said nothing about his interest in Capitú of course. In fact, during the conversation José Dias cautioned him against being too familiar with the Padua family as being the social and moral inferiors of a Santiago, though he conceded that Capitú, if it were not for those eyes of hers—the eyes of a dissembling gypsy— would not be so bad.

The immediate effect of this remark was to send the young man to Padua's house for a better look at Capitú's eyes; this look led by gradual and pleasant degrees to the first kiss.

José Dias had done a good job of awakening Santiago's adolescent sexual impulses and directing them to an object. He did better: he placed an obstacle in the way of his love—the seminary, separation forever, or at least for an indefinite time. Under the impetus of this threat, Capitú and Bento swore eternal love and a solemn oath that they would marry. They then set earnestly, patiently, and slyly about the task of circumventing the obstacle.

Santiago went to the seminary, but with the covert assurance of José Dias that the latter would secure his present release by getting Dona Gloria to send him to Europe to study law. The release came sooner than José Dias expected. Among Santiago's classmates his best friend was Escobar (who was determined to leave the seminary also and go into business). It was he who provided the solution—that Dona Gloria pay for the education of some orphan who would substitute for her son in carrying out her promise. This solution, after the family priest Cabral had got the approval of the bishop, was accepted by Dona Gloria. Bento left the seminary at the age of seventeen, went to São Paulo to study law, and at the end of five years returned with his degree and married Capitú.

This is the rough framework of the first two-thirds of Santiago's tale, but the real story takes place inside Santiago: here we find our Othello.

José Dias not only implanted the seeds of love in Bento by his "informing"; he also implanted the suspicion that Capitú would entrap and deceive him, with the remark about her "gypsy's eyes." While Bento was in the seminary, although he went home on many week ends, José Dias would visit him between times to bring news of the family and to report on progress in breaking down Dona Gloria's resolution. On one of these occasions Bento asked after Capitú. José Dias replied that she was gay and carefree as usual, and added that she would probably "hook" one of the young nobles in the neighborhood and marry him. The thought that Capitú was happy while he was sad and lonesome, and that she was flirting with some handsome noble, turned Santiago's vague feeling of suspicion into definite jealousy.

The title of this chapter is "Uma ponta de Iago" ("A touch of Iago"); from this point on, Othello-Santiago takes over the role of Iago as well, and manipulates his own handkerchiefs to fan his own jealous passion. The erstwhile Iago—José Dias—gradually reverses his opinion of Capitú, works for her happiness and Bento's, and sinks into the role of an amiable busybody who never quite finds out what is going on, and even fails to get his trip to Europe with all expenses paid.

For a few weeks Santiago's floating jealousy fastened on anyone or no one. Then one Sunday Escobar visited him. While Santiago was bidding him many affectionate good-byes and putting him on the omnibus at the front door, Capitú saw Escobar for the first time. He did not see her. She was peeking through the blinds of her front window. As Santiago turned away from the omnibus she called from the window, "What great friend is this?"

At that moment a handsome young man rode by on horseback. He turned in his saddle and looked at Capitú, and Capitú looked at him. The horse went on, but the rider continued to stare back at Capitú.

A delirium of rage came over Santiago, but he was not consciously aware that his jealousy had fixed on Escobar. He thought it was caused by the young dandy who passed on horseback and happened to look at Capitú at almost the same moment she looked at Escobar. It is Santiago the narrator who insinuates that the real object of his jealousy was Escobar. And Escobar was a boy who might easily arouse envy by his own good qualities. He was intelligent, a veritable genius at mathematics and logic; he was muscular; he had ingratiating ways. Santiago's only superiority to Escobar (in Santiago's opinion) consisted in his being the only son of a holy, wealthy, and aristocratic mother. Escobar's mother was dead; he was poor.

Shortly before Santiago and Capitú married, Escobar married Capitú's best friend, Sancha. The two young couples were inseparable. Escobar went into the coffee trade and made money; he got Santiago his first legal cases. Santiago's attacks of jealousy continued without interruption. On his honeymoon it seemed to him that Capitú was anxious to go back to

Rio de Janeiro. When he took her to balls, men stared at her beautiful arms. At home, if her attention wandered for a second, he suspected her thoughts; if she gazed out to sea, he was jealous of the sea. So far as the reader knows, he was not conscious that Escobar was the object of his jealousy. Santiago the narrator, meanwhile, by his subtle insinuations, piles up evidence against Escobar and Capitú.

Two years after their marriage Santiago and Capitú had a son, Ezekiel, who almost from babyhood displayed a talent for mimicking those about him—among others, Escobar. In Santiago's eyes Ezekiel actually resembled Escobar; as he grew older the resemblance grew. Though Santiago explained away the resemblance with rationalizations, and noted that every act, word, and gesture of both Capitú and Escobar demonstrated their innocence, at the same time his latent suspicion somehow converted these very proofs into fuel to feed his smoldering jealousy—until the reader too begins to believe in their guilt.

Then one night Santiago gazed into Sancha's eyes and held her hand. He fancied that she returned his interest as well as the pressure of his hand, and he planned to make serious advances to her later. The next morning Escobar (a powerful swimmer) was drowned in a heavy surf. Santiago was left substitute executor of his estate: everything in the dead man's effects—in his will, in the letter he left for Santiago—pointed to his devotion to his friend and his innocence of any disloyalty. Again Santiago's jealousy interpreted this evidence in its own way, and so reasonably that the reader is inclined to go along with him in his suspicions.

Because Sancha was overwhelmed with grief at the loss of her husband, Santiago began to mistrust his interpretation of her feelings toward himself; his envy of Escobar increased. At the funeral, when Capitú was trying gently to pull the grief-stricken Sancha away

8

from the coffin, she too looked down at the corpse. "There was a moment when Capitú's eyes stared at the dead man . . . great and wide like the swollen wave of the sea beyond, as if she too wished to swallow up the swimmer of that morning." As Santiago watched, his jealousy broke through into his consciousness and beyond restraint.

He could no longer brook the sight of Ezekiel (now seven years old), and sent him to boarding school. He stayed away from home. And his thoughts ran on revenge day and night. Strangling was too good for Capitú, because she was guilty, not innocent like Desdemona: What if Desdemona had been as guilty as Capitú? What death would the Moor have conceived for her? "A bolster would not suffice; there would be need of blood and fire, a vast, intense fire to consume her wholly, and reduce her to dust, and the dust tossed to the wind, in external extinction . . ." He tried to poison himself, he tried to poison Ezekiel; but his hand drew back, partly because he was a nineteenth-century Brazilian, Christian, and Catholic, partly because he had thought of a more refined, a more cruel revenge.

Suddenly he became a man of action. He made his accusations to Capitú. ("Even dead men," murmured Capitú. "Not even the dead escape your jealousy!") He took Capitú and Ezekiel to Switzerland and left them there, far from home, friends, family, far from him. To her affectionate and homesick letters he answered coldly and briefly. She asked him to come to see her. He went to Europe repeatedly. When friends and family asked after her, he answered as if he had seen her—but he never saw her. At home he took mistresses, but they could not make him forget Capitú. Nevertheless, as he tells us rather frequently, he "ate well" and "did not sleep badly."

One day Ezekiel, now grown, came to see him. "Oh, yes," remarks Santiago to the reader, "I believe I neglected to mention that Capitú was dead and buried.

She was. She reposes there in the old country, in Switzerland." Like Desdemona, she died praising her Othello. Ezekiel was anxious to see his father, because Capitú had spoken much of him, praised him as "the finest man in the world and the most worthy of being loved." To Santiago, Ezekiel appeared neither more nor less than his old schoolmate risen from the grave; he was glad to pay the expenses of an archæological expedition to the Near East to be rid of Ezekiel. Yet he grumbled to himself: "One of the consequences of the stolen love of the father is that I pay his son money for his archæology. I would rather pay him with a case of leprosy." Santiago was horrified at his own wish, but a year later, on receiving word of Ezekiel's death from cholera, he "ate a good dinner and went to the theater."

The conclusion to which Santiago gradually leads the reader is that the deceit perpetrated against him by his dearly loved wife and dearly loved friend wrought upon him and changed him from the kind, loving, ingenuous Bento into the hard, cruel, and cynical Dom Casmurro.

2

The Handkerchief of Desdemona

THIS IS SANTIAGO'S STORY—his betrayal by his wife and his best friend. But Machado de Assis (in contrast to his creature Santiago) was not in the habit of writing novels of intrigue. The basis of his novels, as he stated on more than one occasion, was to display the drama resulting from interplay of contrasting natures.[1] He evidently believed that this was the *only* basis for a story. In his famous criticism of Eça de Queiroz's *Primo Basílio*[2] and the naturalistic school, he states this belief in no uncertain terms:

> The substitution of the accessory for the principal, the transferring of the action from the nature and feelings of the characters to the incidental and fortuitous, seems to me incompatible with and contrary to the laws of art . . . Desdemona's handkerchief plays a big part in her death; but the hot, jealous soul of Othello, the perfidy of Iago, and the innocence of Desdemona—these are the principal elements of the action. The drama exists because it is in the natures, in the passions, in the spiritual condition of the characters: the accessory does not control the absolute; it, like Boileau's *rhyme* "ne doit qu'obéir."

Santiago tells us that the big difference between his story and Othello's is that Capitú was guilty. But is there not a more obvious difference, one that arises

11

from Santiago's own nature? The "accessory"—the "handkerchief of Desdemona"—in *Dom Casmurro* is the resemblance, or fancied resemblance, of Ezekiel to Escobar. Santiago's putative Iago, José Dias, had abandoned the role long before this resemblance made its appearance. It was Santiago who discovered the resemblance; it was Santiago who manipulated this "handkerchief." We must reword Machado's formula for dramatic action to read: the jealous soul of Othello-Santiago, the perfidy of Iago-Santiago, and the guilt (or innocence) of Desdemona-Capitú—these are the principal elements of the action. The drama exists because it is in the natures, passions, and spiritual condition of Othello-Santiago, Iago-Santiago, and Desdemona-Capitú; the resemblance between Ezekiel and Escobar does not control these three characters, from whose passions the action flows.

Let us examine the three "principal elements" in *Dom Casmurro* and compare them with their counterparts in *Othello*. Since the guilt or innocence of Capitú depends entirely upon the testimony of Santiago, whose jealousy alone renders that testimony suspect, I shall postpone the Desdemona element to later chapters and take up here only the Othello and Iago elements.

It is true, as Santiago relates, that José Dias started as an Iago; but he was at best a poor kind of Iago, one of humble ambitions, and not much interested in money: food and lodging, an occasional ticket to the theater, a trip to Europe, and the admiration of the Santiago household—this was all he asked of life. Though his envy of the influence of the Padua family led him to "inform" on Capitú and Bento and thus hasten the seminary for Bento, the conniving of the young Desdemona and Othello easily won him to their side—first to getting Bento out of the seminary, then to promoting the marriage. It was probably this same envy that prompted him to remark on Capitú's "gypsy's eyes" and on Padua's scheming to marry into the Santiago family, and to say that Capitú had her cap set for one of the young aristocrats of the neighborhood. With this last remark his power as a thoroughgoing Iago disappeared, and he slipped into his role of an amiable busybody working for the happiness of the Santiago clan. Shakespeare's Iago says to Cassio, "In following him [Othello], I follow but myself."[3] José Dias actually carried out this purpose: he came to identify himself with the Santiago family—their welfare and happiness became his. The "married couple of sin and virtue" that Santiago says is in each one of us fighting for control of our lives was in José Dias self-love and devotion to his patrons—and the latter won out. (In Santiago there was a similar struggle, but the outcome, we shall find, was quite different.)

Long before José Dias had cast aside the mantle of Iago, Santiago was preparing to snatch it up. As he was quick to recognize the truth of José Dias's suggestion that he and Capitú were in love, so he was equally quick to believe that she was tricky and that Padua was scheming to marry into the wealthy and aristocratic Santiago family. He went further, and involved Capitú's mother, Dona Fortunata, in his suspicions. When Dona Fortunata came upon the young lovers after the kiss, Santiago tells us

> she looked at us with gentleness . . . Then, I think, she had a doubt or two . . . she suspected that perhaps there had been something more than combing hair between us, and she smiled and pretended not to notice . . .

Twice in the quarrel scene Dona Fortunata appeared, but went away without saying anything, although the second time Bento had his arm around Capitú's waist.

Santiago's suspicion of Padua was more gross, though the first suggestions are quiet and unobtrusive: the relation of José Dias's insinuations, the obsequiousness of Padua to his young neighbor. In the procession of the Blessed Sacrament, when Padua was asked to yield

13

the pole of the canopy to him, Santiago remarks: "It was putting a father's heart to the test . . . 'All right, I'll give it up to our Bentinho,' sighed Capitú's father." Santiago scoffs at Padua's tenderness toward him on the eve of the departure for the seminary, and discounts Padua's tears as arising from self-interest—despair at the loss of his hope of having Santiago for a son-in-law: "His face wore a disenchanted look, like a man who has spent his whole hoard of hopes on a single lottery ticket and sees the cursed number come out a blank— such a sweet number!" The same image and the same idea are repeated in Santiago's dream.[4] And finally, note the callous manner in which he announces the death of Padua: "All went well . . . all went well. I had lost my father-in-law, it is true . . ."[5]

In the early chapters José Dias is sketched (by Santiago) as a sly, self-seeking, officious troublemaker. Though his later actions demonstrate that he had turned harmless, well-meaning, solicitous, and devoted, Santiago's suspicions of him persisted. As a boy he attributed José Dias's willingness to help him out of the seminary to slyness and insincerity—a device to ingratiate himself with the future master. Even José Dias's apparent joy in the marriage—accepted as real by Capitú and Bento at the time—has doubt cast upon it by the insinuation of Santiago the narrator that in their happiness the young couple did not question that which was decidedly questionable: "Happiness is a kindly soul."[6] In the next chapter he reminds us that José Dias was a sponger alternating breakfasts at his house with dinners at Dona Gloria's. Even at the end, in the chapter in which José Dias dies, Santiago still cannot relinquish his doubts: "Perhaps he hoped to bury me . . . Thus he prepared to take care of the third generation, but death came before Ezekiel."

Santiago's account of Escobar is Iago's account of Cassio, softened and misted over with Othello's early

14

trust in and affection for his old camp mate who went "a-wooing with him."

Iago says of Cassio that he is "a great arithmetician," a "Florentine" (that is, given to insincere courtesy and flattery, and a businessman); a "counter-caster"; bookish; a voluble and smooth talker; handsome, with handsome manners; just the type to please women, and therefore to be suspected; a "hypocritical, designing knave"; rash and choleric, especially in drink.[7] Only the last attribute is spared Escobar by Santiago. For the rest, the two evaluations are almost identical. Consider the first description of Escobar: he was a shifty-eyed boy with shifty feet and shifty hands; he was jolly, reflective, and hypocritical ("He always explained that he was meditating upon some spiritual point"); he had a good memory, but "perhaps this faculty robbed some other"; he came from Curitiba—which, like Florence, was noted for leather working and as a city of tradesmen, but also, as Florence was noted as the birthplace of Machiavelli, Curitiba was practically founded by the Jesuits. Santiago suggests that Escobar was scheming to marry him to his sister, and that he wormed his way into his confidence.[8] Escobar was polite, talkative, with good manners, flattering, handsome (though his forehead may have been too low). His chosen field was commerce, and, as we discover later, he was successful in it. He was a great arithmetician; he cleverly discovered how many houses Dona Gloria owned, and later got her to finance him in business. His sharp practices are again hinted in his amusement over the child Ezekiel's advantageous distribution of unwanted sweets and in his laughing offer to make Ezekiel his business partner.

It is not only to Escobar that Santiago attributes an excessive interest in money; there are Capitú with her Caesar's pearl and her ten pounds sterling, Padua, José Dias, and perhaps even Cousin Justina. But how about Santiago?

15

Iago accuses Cassio of being a "counter-caster," when it is he—Iago—who is putting Roderigo's money in his purse. Iago's lines constantly allude to the subject of money. So Santiago, in addition to suspecting everyone about him of having an eye on his family's fortune, was forever talking of money. He reduced the most sacred relationships with God and man to the lingo of the money mart—buying, selling, lending, and winning in a lottery. At a tender age he began to buy Heaven's favors by using prayers as currency; when he got behind in his payments, he mortgaged his soul;[9] kept renewing and increasing the mortgage until, in a desperate appeal, he persuaded God to cancel the debt and make a new contract putting their trading on a cash basis.[10] Even in his prayers for a son he "paid in advance like house rent."[11] Virtues, he tells us, are real property and may be hocked in Purgatory, which "is a pawnshop that lends on all the virtues, for high interest and short term. But the term may be renewed until, one day, one or two middling virtues pay for all one's sins great and small."[12] Even "the unintentional virtues" have a cash value according to Santiago's theories of interplanetary finance.[13] He attributes the same type of dealings with Heaven to his mother, who (he says) "extended her note with her multimillionaire Creditor" and, when the inevitable day of reckoning came, used "intention" for money.[14] Note too his extravagant admiration for Escobar's way with figures, and the summing of the house rents, which caused him to hug Escobar and call him friend.[15] In the same way, his tender emotions were aroused by Capitú's ten pounds [16] and by her command not to buy jewelry for her.[17] His emotions of love were "golden" ideas.[18] Death—really murder—was better than prize money; it does not "dribble away."[19] If Capitú should prove innocent of infidelity, he was willing not to *pardon* her but to make *"reparation"*—that is, to pay her damages (the italics are Santiago's).[20] No—Santiago was concerned

16

with money; but, as Iago called Cassio a "counter-caster," he says of Escobar: "We would go down to the beach . . . —he given over to his calculations, I to my dreams."[21]

And Santiago's Escobar, like Iago's Cassio, was born to seduce women: we have seen how handsome and ingratiating he was; Santiago also hints of an affair with an actress or dancer, just as Iago pointed up the Cassio-Bianca relationship. Throughout his life Santiago-Othello found Escobar a good friend. Yet even at the beginning of their friendship the other Santiago—Santiago-Iago—suspected that he might not have been sincere, and his suspicions continued to grow.

Santiago's suspicions of Capitú are the warp of his narrative. It was Santiago who attributed to Capitú the "supersubtle" quality that Iago attributes to Desdemona. She was "reflective"; her ways were "apt" and "sinuous."[22] With cold calculation she laid a carefully thought out plan. Her rearrangement of the formula of their oath of fidelity is attributed by Santiago to the subtlety of her reasoning and scheming—not to her great love. On their honeymoon he interpreted her eagerness to get back to the city and show her new estate as an indication that she had married him for wealth and position. In the chapter "Doubts on doubts" he refers to the "fine art" of Capitú twice within three paragraphs, and the same phrase is used a few chapters later.[23] It is Santiago who insinuates—like Iago repeating Brabantio's warning "She has deceiv'd her father, and may thee"—but Santiago's insinuation is more inclusive: she has deceived both her father and her mother, and everyone else, and so may thee. One could go on quoting endlessly. Her superior powers in the way of deceit are constantly remarked by Santiago—and envied.[24] He sums up his view in the final chapter: she was deceitful by nature, deceitful to the core. In the same chapter he sums up the action for us: the beloved wife and the beloved friend—two deceitful natures—joined forces to deceive an open, frank, generous, blindly loving and gullible nature—an Othello as easily "led by the nose as asses are."

We have noted that Santiago "envied" Capitú her powers of dissimulation. There is perhaps a question whether his envy on this head was entirely justified, but more of that later. For the present let us merely establish that he was not exactly averse to trifling with the truth on occasion. Recall the attitude in which we first find him, behind the door, eavesdropping. In reporting what he heard to Capitú he left out José Dias's "informing," but perhaps, as he says, this was natural from an adolescent shyness. He went along with Capitú's deceitful plan willingly and cleverly enough, and came to admire it and enjoy his part in it. He was secretive with Justina, Padua, his mother, and José Dias. When he admitted to Capitú that he loved her more than his mother, Capitú called him a "liar": the reader knows that the night before he had told his mother that he loved only her.

He was given to half-truths. He explained his visit to Sancha's house "with the absolute truth"—that is, as having been his mother's suggestion; but what actually made him go was Justina's insinuation that Capitú was there flirting with a young man. He told his mother that he sometimes dreamed of angels and saints, but it was Capitú who did this.[25] After relating one of his lies to Capitú, he begs the reader, "Don't call me deceitful, call me compassionate."[26] He reproached Capitú with forgetting their love song (the peddler's song), but he too had forgotten it.

After his jealousy of Escobar broke into the open his deceits became definite and calculated. He lied to Capitú about his money affairs—to torture her and test her devotion. He disguised his feelings toward the child Ezekiel and lied to him about visiting him at boarding school. When Ezekiel returned as a young man, Santiago deliberately assumed "a fatherly air."

He tricked Justina out of seeing Ezekiel. He made trips to Europe for the sole purpose of giving the impression that he visited Capitú, though he never went near her or had any intention of doing so.

Iago stuck at nothing in the way of deceit. This is not true of Santiago, who had a conscience that often asserted itself. He was overcome with remorse after the wish for his mother's death. Even when old and "casmurro," he was horrified by his thought that he would rather give Ezekiel "leprosy" than the money he was actually giving him. There was a tussle with his conscience over his advances to Sancha. And when he broke his oath and forgot the peddler's tune, he went into an elaborate rationalization to explain his lapse. To come back to our initial point, Santiago is not a pure Iago: Iago and Othello are both in him. Critics of Shakespeare have interpreted Iago as "the evil which is in every one of us,"[27] and as a personification of the suspicion and jealousy in Othello.[28] Santiago himself indicates his difficulty, with the explanation of his theory of good and evil. In each person there are sins and virtues paired in married couples. When one partner in the marriage is stronger than the other, it alone guides the individual; but usually they both control—now one, now the other, or even both simultaneously.[29] In other words, suspicion, vanity, sensuality, and hate were vying with trust, candor, generosity, and love for domination of the man. In Shakespeare's play, Othello's love was attacked from without by Iago's envy, hatred, and deceit. In *Dom Casmurro,* the struggle took place within the one man.

To throw further light on the nature of this struggle, let us briefly examine Machado de Assis's first novel, *Resurreição,* which seems to contain the germ of *Dom Casmurro. Resurreição* is also an adaptation of *Othello* to the contemporary Brazilian scene, but it is a novice's attempt. It was written twenty-eight years earlier, when Machado's art was not yet capable of

19

the legerdemain found in *Dom Casmurro*, so that the characters are not the subtly complex human beings of the later novel. They are somewhat wooden and consistent; though partly rounded, each presents one dominant façade—which makes them easier to understand. Further, this novel is narrated by Machado de Assis—not by a fictional personage—and the explanatory asides of the author are earnest and outspoken, so that his message is made quite clear.

3

The Germ

THE THEME OF *Resurreição* is doubt—doubt of self,
which engenders suspicion of others. Machado de
Assis stated in his preface:

> My idea in writing this book was to put into action
> that thought of Shakespeare's:
>> "Our doubts are traitors,
>> And make us lose the good we oft might win,
>> By fearing to attempt."
>
> I had no intention of composing a novel of man-
> ners but only the sketch of a situation and the
> throwing into contrast of two natures; with these
> simple ingredients I have sought to create the
> book's interest.

The same theme of doubt is restated, along with the
quotation from Shakespeare, on the final page of the
novel.

The title *Resurrection* explains the action: a man's
dead "heart" or "capacity for love" came to life in the
warming flame of a woman's love, then sank back into
the tomb again, snuffed out by jealousy. The jealousy
was engendered and fed by "desconfiança." (Portuguese dictionaries define "desconfiança" as a lack of
trust, fear of being deceived, the disposition of one who
doubts the honesty or sincerity of others, who is easily
offended, carries a chip on his shoulder, takes general

remarks or jokes as personal affronts, who has no confidence in himself or in others.)

The story may be summed up as follows. Felix, a
wealthy, well-educated man-about-town, given to casual
affairs with young ladies of the upper demimonde,
but still a thoughtful, cultivated young man of refined
speech and natural, unassuming manners, was attracted
by the voluptuous beauty and warmth of a wealthy
young widow Livia. Though Livia encouraged him to
call, he avoided her until once when he helped her into
a carriage he imagined that she meaningfully pressed
his hand. We *know* he imagined it, because Machado
de Assis tells us so. Felix got the mistaken idea that
she was ready to have an affair with him. He began to
court her, but only for pastime and with no serious
intentions.

The widow, with her faith, unconcealed admiration,
and love, soon made him wonder if he had mistaken
her intention. He asked himself if she might not affect
his fate more than he then imagined, and if from this
caprice of the moment might not result the ruin of his
whole life. His love, animated by that of Livia, took
away his pleasure in the conquest.

> What did his heart mean by thrusting itself into
> this episode which had to be short to be beautiful,
> which should have neither past nor future, nor
> raptures nor tears! . . . "What can I give her in
> return for her love? My mind, perhaps, gentleness,
> affection, only these . . . because love . . . I
> love? Place my whole existence in the hands of an-
> other . . . more than existence, destiny . . .
> what do I know of such things?"[1]

A few seconds later "desconfiança" engendered doubts
of the purity of the widow's love:

> "I believe she feels the same way I do. I should
> have known. She speaks with great passion; but
> she probably knows her art; she's a colorist. Other-
> wise she would seem to be surrendering out of

curiosity, perhaps from habit. A mad passion can justify a sin: she's getting ready to commit an indiscretion. Hasn't she been trying to seduce me all this while? It's sure; the fact is staring me in the face. And I imagined . . ."

[Felix] was completely convinced that the widow's attentiveness was a mixture of vanity, caprice, and sensual inclination. And this, to him, was to be preferred to a disinterested and sincere passion—in which, what is more, he had no faith.

Time, habit, and Livia's loyal love and belief in his love, temporarily laid his doubts. He proposed marriage. But the old "desconfiança" was still there, distilling jealousies that attacked his newborn love.

Felix's love had a bitter taste, for it was laced with doubt and suspicion. Livia had called him "touchy," and rightly. The fall of a rose petal bruised him. A smile, a glance, a gesture—anything—was enough to darken his mood. The girl's very thoughts did not escape his suspicions. If he detected the listlessness of reflection in her gaze, he began to conjure up causes, recalling a gesture of the evening before, a half-explained look, an obscure and ambiguous phrase; and all these things fused in the poor lover's mind, and shaped themselves into the girl's faithlessness, real and clear.[2]

Felix's "desconfiança" even drove him to tempt Livia with another man.

One word from [Felix] would have sufficed to remove this budding rival from his path. Felix rejected the idea half from calculation half from pride—silly pride but natural to him. The calculation was a worse thing: it was a trap—test he called it—to throw them together . . . and weigh Livia's constancy and sincerity.

Thus he was the artificer of his own wretchedness, with his own hands he placed together the fuel for the fire in which he was to roast, if not in reality, at least in fantasy; for, where no evil existed before, he would draw it out of the void and give it life and action.[3]

But Livia's love, which was proof against all this, continued to revive and animate Felix's heart until the Iago of the story, a Dr. Baptista who wanted the wealthy widow for himself, took definite steps to kill it once more.

Machado leaves us in no doubt as to the character of this villain. He was a model of dissimulation and calculation.[4] He was given to coarse wit.[5] He was sensual. He was observant and cunning, without passions and scruples.[6] He laid a plan to

> multiply [Felix's] suspicions, plant the canker of jealousy deep in his heart, make him the instrument of his own destruction. He did not adopt Iago's method, which seemed to him risky and puerile: instead of injecting suspicion through the ears, he infected his eyes.[7]

Baptista's "poison" was an anonymous letter about Livia sent to Felix on the eve of the day set for the wedding. Felix immediately wrote a letter to Livia breaking off the marriage. Though he acted on impulse, he was convinced that the information in the anonymous letter was true. Within a few days, by reading and rereading the letter, he convinced himself that he had acted justly, and "his heart became quiet." He had returned to his normal, placid existence when he was visited by his friend Menezes. Menezes showed him that he had acted unreasonably and inspired him with the suspicion that the anonymous letter was the work of Baptista. Here is what Machado de Assis has to say:

> Let us understand each other, reader. I, who am telling this story, can assure you that the letter really was the work of Luiz Baptista. But [Felix's] conviction, though surely sincere, was less well

grounded and less well considered than it should have been. His heart gave way to the caprice of a new "desconfiança." . . . He was now all love and hatred, repentance and revenge.[8]

But Livia sadly refused to marry Felix, with this explanation:

"It's no use. Your evil genius will pursue you, Felix. Your mind will breed clouds to darken our sky. Your doubts will follow you wherever we go, because they dwell eternally in your heart . . . Let us love from a distance. Let us be each to the other a luminous trail from the past which indelibly crosses time and makes golden and warm the dark mists of old age."[9]

The last chapter of the book is the author's report ten years later. Livia has been living in a nunlike retirement, devoting herself to the education of her son.

Even today she has not forgotten the chosen one of her heart, and as time goes on she spiritualizes and sanctifies the memory of the past. The wrongs of Felix are forgotten; the luminous trail of which she spoke at their last meeting is all that is left for her. . . .

Felix was not one to shut himself up in a cloister. The sad impression left by the events which the reader has witnessed—if it overwhelmed him— rapidly disappeared. Love went out like a lamp that lacks oil. It was the presence of [Livia] which fed the flame: when that presence was removed the feeble flame sputtered and died. . . . [His] love had posthumous doubts. The truth of the letter which had prevented the marriage, with the passing of time, not only appeared possible to him, but even probable. When Menezes told him one day that he had absolute proof that Luiz Baptista had written it, Felix did not reject the evidence nor ask for the proof. What he believed in his inmost soul was that Baptista's villainy did not

25

exclude the likelihood of its being true, and that was enough to convince him.

The widow's austere and solitary life could not escape his suspicious observation. At first he believed in it. After a little he began to doubt that it was purely a retirement; he came to believe, rather, that it was a clever concealment.

Blessed with everything that society could give him to make him happy, Felix is essentially unhappy. Nature placed him in that class of pusillanimous and visionary men described by the poet's reflection, "They lose the good by fearing to attempt." Not content with the felicity which lapped him round, he yearns for that inner felicity of everlasting, soul-satisfying love. He will never attain it, because his heart, if it rose from the dead for a few days, has forgotten in the tomb its feeling of trust and its moments of fleeting ecstasy.

Superficial resemblances between this novel and *Dom Casmurro* cannot fail to strike the reader. But in this early novel Machado's characters, though a trifle wooden—or for that very reason—are clear-cut. There is no question of his Iago's villainy, no question of Desdemona's faithful love, no question of the flaw in his Othello. Felix, blessed with wealth, a good education, refined tastes, and with the loyal love of a good and beautiful woman, was prevented from enjoying this love by his "desconfiança," which engendered jealous doubts. Santiago traced his doubts and suspicions to a factual cause—Capitú's betrayal as definitely proved to him by Ezekiel's resemblance to Escobar. Felix's "desconfiança" existed independently and in spite of anything Livia did. As we have seen, the author speaks frankly to the reader and warns him that Felix's reasoning and arguments are untrustworthy. We cannot but wonder how the story would read if Felix had narrated it, as Santiago did his.

The short stories "Miss Dollar" (in which the heroine suspects her suitors of being after her money) and "A

26

Segunda Vida" (part of the hero's lunacy is fear of being married for his money) also demonstrate that Machado de Assis regarded "desconfiança" as a mental aberration. Felix intimated that his "desconfiança" was the effect of a disastrous love affair:[10] he had "embraced a serpent"; before that he had "confiança." As he says to Livia,

> "No one lost his heart more generously than I . . . no one knew better than I how to be friend and lover. I was credulous like you; hypocrisy, perfidy, egoism never seemed to me anything but pitiable aberrations."[11]

But Machado warns us against Felix's explanation, and adds:

> Distrust of his own feelings and those of others did not only come from the disillusionments he had suffered; it was rooted in mobility of spirit and faintness of heart. His energy was an act of will, not an inborn quality; he was above all else weak and changeable.

Felix's "desconfiança" was inborn. Machado's explanations to the reader go no deeper than that; but there are hints, in his descriptions of Felix's emotions and actions, of another cause. One of the characters in the book says of Felix that he was one of the few young men who would talk to older women even though there were young ladies present. Felix's love of Livia was genuinely aroused for the first time when he discovered that she had a six-year-old son, who ran up to her as she was talking to Felix.

> During this scene, Felix seemed completely abstracted from everything around him. He did not hear the gentle scolding of the young woman nor the prattling of the child; he heard only himself. He contemplated that picture with a pleasurable envy tinged with remorse.
> "She's a mother," he kept repeating to himself, "she's a mother!"
> . . . Felix gazed at her with religious respect

. . . He kissed her ardently, but he could say nothing. His emotion stifled his voice; his thoughts imposed silence . . .

A vague, faraway idea arose in his imagination and took him on a long excursion into the land of memory.[12]

With the boy Luiz, Felix also became a child, "expansive, garrulous, tender, almost infantile."[13]

These hints are vague and not followed up—there is no mention anywhere in the book of Felix's mother—but they *are* hints.

Santiago's love for his mother is no hint; it is a fact established time and again. And the pattern for betrayal by a woman was set by her: she sacrificed him to God. Santiago himself consciously acknowledged this betrayal when he compared her to Abraham sacrificing Isaac.[14] From the first, Capitú recognized the strength of this love for his mother. When Bento told her that José Dias had reminded his mother of her promise and urged her to send him to the seminary at once, Capitú's anger exploded, not against José Dias, but against Dona Gloria. And note Santiago's reaction: He was hurt and confused by Capitú's outburst, and relieved when she apologized. In this same scene Capitú showed her lack of confidence in Santiago's vows that he would resist and not enter the seminary: "You," she said contemptuously, "you will enter"; and she prepared an elaborate, long-drawn-out strategy, because she knew the force that they—she and Bento —were up against: his attachment to his mother. Consider their first quarrel, caused by Capitú's doubt of Bento's love for her: she began by questioning his courage to endure danger and hardship for their love. These questions naturally puzzled Bento, and apparently Capitú herself did not quite understand them. Then the real cause of her doubt came into the open, with her series of questions beginning: "If you had to choose between your mother and me which would you choose?" When Bento finally replied that he would choose Capitú, she called him a liar—with some justice as we have already observed. And note his reaction to Capitú's insulting epithet: All right, he would go back to his mother, become a priest, abandon her, and as a priest marry her to another man. But when Capitú threatened to do what his mother had done—that is, have a child by this other man—a strange feeling of complete loss and chaos came over him.

Santiago's problem was, however, not simply one of a strong mother attachment. One must consider the nature of his mother—at least in the young Bento's eyes. She was a "saint,"[15] as innocent as Eve before the Fall.[16] God sent her a son, which she was to return to Him by previous agreement. If anyone doubts that Machado de Assis was capable of inserting into the subconscious of this sensitive boy the belief that he was the son of God by the Virgin Mary, it is only necessary to recall the hard-headed, successful banker Santos of *Esaú e Jacob* who *consciously* believed that he was the father of two reincarnated Apostles.[17] The young Santiago had every reason to believe that there was something special about him and his mother. José Dias likened her to the Virgin on more than one occasion;[18] Escobar called her "saint" and a "double angel";[19] Padre Cabral and the rector of the seminary regarded Santiago's birth as a "miracle."[20] Santiago tells us that he himself was incapable of lying,[21] that he was pure[22] before he came to love Capitú with her "eyes that the devil had given her."[23] To him Capitú represented the opposite of his mother: her eyes were a treacherous sea drawing him into its dark depths.[24] Machado de Assis was not unfamiliar with the Greek myth that Venus was born of the sea.[25] To Santiago the tide in Capitú's eyes was a projection of his own adolescent sexual urge, which frightened him. He was caught between love for his mother—which, because of her divine connections, was holy, spiritual, and

Christlike—and profane, carnal love. Born into and brought up in his snug little holy family, he was being drawn into the world of the flesh and the devil.

Though Santiago loved his mother, there were moments when he hated her—for her devotion to God the Father, her willingness to sacrifice him to God. He wished her dead; he had an urge to hurt her by telling her in detail of his love and courtship of Capitú; he got an exquisite delight out of deceiving her with Capitú—her and her houseful of sanctimonious toadies. In the same way, he loved God his indulgent Father, of whom he expected every boon as a son's right, and was willing and eager to be His adoring priest; but at times he hated Him too, was irreverent and blasphemous, made fun of His servants, tried to cheat and trick Him. He envied God not only his mother's devotion but also Capitú's. For his putative father, Pedro Santiago de Albuquerque, he showed little emotion; *he* was, for the most part, only a kind of saint on an altar, a figurehead adding luster to the holiness of the family.

As Santiago tells it, there was a certain amount of struggle going on in Dona Gloria between her love for her son and her love for God; but it was not much of a struggle, because she had not much to lose— only his absence of a few years at the seminary, after which he would come home to live with her again. In this absence, however, and even before, an interesting phenomenon occurred: Dona Gloria began to identify herself with Capitú.[26] Capitú became one of the holy family. Dona Gloria was willing and eager to go along with Bento in cheating God with a casuistical trick, and gave her son to Capitú as to a part of herself.

This same identification of Capitú with his mother and their holy family evidently took place in Santiago's mind as well. Capitú is likened to an altar before which he, as priest, worshiped; the house he planned for them was to be located on a quiet street like his mother's, and it was to have an oratory to "Our Lady of the Immaculate Conception"; they were married in heaven with all kinds of special dispensations and attentions from St. Peter and the heavenly choir; they went to live in the Rua da Gloria.

For a time there was a certain amnesty with Heaven. Then the devil, or destiny, began to exact his own. For Santiago was Santiago, and under the pressures of life his "desconfiança"—created by his love and hatred for his mother—engendered doubts, suspicion, and jealousy, which finally made him incapable of loving anyone. He tried to return as a little boy to his mother, and to keep her completely for himself he cut off her memory from others with an anonymous tombstone: "Who will care about dates, filiation, or even names, after I am gone?" He sent Capitú and the rest of the world to the devil. But, to satisfy his ambivalence, he placed before him the portraits of both his mother and father, called them a devoted couple, and deceived his mother (and Capitú) with women of the streets.

Santiago is correct in believing that he was torn between the forces of good and evil, but he is not quite correct in believing that these forces were embodied, respectively, in his mother and Capitú. The irony is not that he was deceived by Capitú, but that he was deceived by himself.

4

What's in a Name

IT WAS SANTIAGO who wrote his story, but the names of the characters—with the exception of Ezekiel's—were conferred by the real author. They are the one element of the novel that can, with absolute certainty, be laid at Machado's door, and Machado de Assis did not name his characters carelessly. A study of his other novels and tales (as well as *Dom Casmurro*) reveals his practice in the matter. As a general rule, he employs Portuguese surnames harking back to the navigators or to prominent figures of early colonial Brazil. The given names, as might be expected in a Catholic country, are from the Saints' Calendar—and in a very few instances, from the Bible alone. The names of foreigners, of course, form an exception to this rule. But in addition to whatever Luso-Brazilian and Christian-Catholic (or foreign) connotation these names may have, and whatever may be suggested by their very sound, at least one further meaning is suggested one way or another.

Many times a name is the same as, related to, or resembles, a common noun, adjective, or verb, the meaning of which indicates a dominant trait of the fictional personage who bears the name. The less serious the work or the character, the more obvious the meaning of the name. The following examples, in which Machado de Assis gives distinct clues to the name's significance, will serve to illustrate this device. (All these examples observe the general rule for Christian names and surnames.)

The government employee of "Quem Conta um Conto...," Bacharel Plácido ("Bachelor of Laws Placid"), in Machado's own words,

> was his own name turned man. Never did phlegm have a more fervid cult. He was fat, pink-cheeked, slow-moving, and cool. He received the two visitors with the easy condescension of a Placid who was truly placid.

There is also a play on his title "Bachelor": the common noun is used in a figurative sense to mean "babbler." Placid was one of the gossips of the tale who spread, and improved upon, a false rumor. Another of the gossips was named Pires. There have been many Pireses in Portuguese history. Two men of this name are mentioned by Fernão Mendes Pinto as partaking of his adventures in the Far East (1537–1558). Since Fernão Mendes Pinto's narrative is generally regarded as highly colored, there is perhaps a connotation of tall tales clinging to the name.[1] But the common noun "pires" means "saucer" and, figuratively, "an ordinary, inconsequential, pretentious person," which also fits Machado's man. (Other Pireses in his works are of the same ilk.)

The first name of Custódio Marques ("O Astrólogo") is an abbreviated form of "Anjo Custódio" ("guardian angel"). "Marques" is reminiscent of the verb "marcar" ("mark or notice"). Appropriately, Custódio Marques held the office of Inspector of Weights and Measures. He also, unofficially, kept an eye on everybody's personal business—he was a kind of self-appointed custodian, or guardian angel, of public morals. As Machado de Assis comments, ". . . he extended his inspection of weights and measures to the inspection of other men's lives."

"Bacamarte," as a common noun, means, literally

33

and figuratively, "blunderbuss." It is the name of the alienist ("O Alienista") whose strict adherence to the scientific principle not only caused a revolution but also blew up in his own face.

Machado de Assis probably conferred the name "Palha" ("straw") upon one of the principals of *Quincas Borba* because the character was something of a non-entity as a man, with none of the finer feelings. But in addition, there seems to be a connotation of the idiom "dar palha" ("to deceive and exploit").

Braz Cubas (*Memórias Póstumas de Braz Cubas*) himself discusses the lowly origin of his surname, which means "vat." The contempt in which the teaching profession was held is indicated by the name of Braz's schoolteacher Barata ("cockroach"), who had his school on Rua do Piolho ("Louse Street").

The satiric tales and fantasies often have characters who are not of Portuguese blood: the significance of their names is still more obvious. Alpha and Omega ("O Dicionário"), the crack philologists who undertook to reform the dictionary, said of themselves: "We, Alpha and Omega, are designated by our very names for things having to do with language." The eminent Dutch psychiatrist of "O Lapso" was named Jeremiah Halma. The Jeremiah element is explained by Machado himself by reference to the Bible. "Halma" is merely the Portuguese word for "soul" or "psyche," *alma*, spelled with an (unpronounced of course) *h* to give it a Dutch look. The general contempt for learning is again indicated by the place of Halma's residence, which, like Barata's school, was on "Louse Street." Lady Emma Sterling was the true-blue Englishwoman of "O Imortal" who went through hell and high water for her picaresque Portuguese lover. In the same tale the Indian wife's name Maracujá is Tupí for "passion-fruit," and her father's name, Pirajuá, is apparently false Tupí for a kind of fish. Consider also Sarah Hope ("Uma Águia sem Azas"), the English girl with political ambitions—even the "Sarah" has a foreign, Puritan-Protestant ring.

Occasionally Machado de Assis uses names inversely, with ironic intent. The Eugenia (Greek for "well-born") to whom Braz Cubas addressed this thought when he was considering seducing her: "I . . . thinking that you could not belie your blood, your origin . . ."[2] was not only a bastard, and lame from birth, but also, because of the circumstances of her birth, poor into the bargain. Another girl of the same name, in the novel *Helena*, was the object of her father's incestuous attachment from babyhood.

In a very few names, Machado has transposed the letters of a word that the name was intended to suggest. "Far-nohr" for the Pharoah of "Identidade" is one example; another is "Carmo," the name given the character in *Memorial de Ayres* who admittedly was intended as a portrait of his own wife Carolina.[3]

A fifth device employed by Machado de Assis for endowing a name with meaning and color was literary allusion. The name of the second Eugenia mentioned above—Eugenia Camargo of *Helena*—probably contains an allusion not only to the original Greek but also to Eugénie Grandet, whose life was ruined by her father's cold-blooded avarice, just as Eugenia Camargo's promises to be ruined by *her* father's ambition. Perhaps the finest example of Machado's use of literary allusion in names is the high-priced Spanish courtesan Marcella of *Memórias Póstumas de Braz Cubas*—who seems to be a Machadeanized version of the shepherdess of the same name who caused such havoc among the goatherds of Spain, near the Pass of Lapice.

Some names Machado seems to have used only once ("Capitolina" is such a name); others he used a number of times, for different characters in different stories, or even in the same story. When a name is thus used repeatedly, we should be able, by comparison of the natures of its bearers, to form some idea of its import. Take for example the old Portuguese surname "Oliveira," which Machado de Assis used for seven different characters in as many short stories.

The first of these, a minor character of an early tale,[4] does not bear any appreciable relationship to Machado's other Oliveiras; but the remaining six are brothers under the skin—that is, faithful old dogs, either as friends or lovers, or both. The prime example is the Oliveira of "Almas Agradecidas," who helped out an old schoolmate only to have the latter abuse his friendship to raise himself economically and socially, and to steal Oliveira's sweetheart. Even so, Oliveira remained a firm friend to both former schoolmate and former sweetheart. In "A Mágoa do Infeliz Cosme," Cosme took advantage of his friend Oliveira's dumb, distant, and respectful devotion to Cosme's wife by selling Oliveira one of the dead wife's jewels—at cost, he said. The Oliveira of "Um Quarto de Século," after twenty-five years of waiting, married the dream of his youth: she did not make him happy. The fourth ("Primas de Sapucaia!"), tied to a "basilisk," nevertheless remained faithful, apparently to death. The fifth ("Cinco Mulheres") was a model husband to a faithless wife. Only in "Um Sonho e Outro Sonho" did the Oliveira tradition pay off: in this story a faithful and persistent lover named Oliveira succeeded in marrying the girl with no indication of ill effects.

From just what source Machado derived the feeling permeating these six Oliveiras is matter for speculation. (The common noun "oliveira" means "olive tree.") Perhaps it was the Bible—"I am like a green olive tree in the house of God: I trust in the mercy of God for ever and ever."[5] Perhaps it was Bartolomeu dos Martyres.

> Some are compared to olive trees loaded with olives. Those are the ones in whom shine charity and mercy, of whom Holy Writ says, "These are

36

the pillars of mercy, whose virtues live always in everlasting memory." We sinners gather the fruit of their branches when we seek to accomplish works of mercy according to our poor abilities.[6] Perhaps the allusion is to Gil Vincente;[7] if so, "oliveira" has the meaning "whipping boy." Or there may be allusion to all three sources or to their basic concept that the olive tree, being evergreen and long-lived, is a perfect symbol for faithfulness. Of one thing we can be reasonably sure: these six Oliveiras did have the traits of doglike devotion and forgiveness in superlative degree.

And if we are tempted to imagine that Machado de Assis used these and other names without premeditation and purpose, we have his own words to confute us. "It is common knowledge, [he writes in one of his columns] that names have great power. There are cases in which they are everything."[8] Again: "One way or another the influence of names is certain." And he adds that if the reader doubts it he has only to pick up Suetonius, and for "Messalina" read "Anastasia" and observe how pale Suetonius' tale of horror, scandal, and nauseating filth will become.[9] In a third column he declares that names have inescapable fates, histories, and connotations.[10]

The allusions clinging to the names in *Dom Casmurro* are subtle, complicated, and various, like the natures of the persons who bear them. The general practice explained above is closely adhered to. The surnames, with the exception of Padua's and the foreigner Marcolini's, hark back to the Portuguese navigators and early Brazil; all the given names are to be found in the Saints' Calendar. The presence of these two elements, though natural, is important to the plot, for they sum up the inheritance of the characters. In the words of Edgar Prestage, "Portugal owes her place in history to three achievements: the opening of the ocean routes, the colonization of Brazil (a land larger

37

than the United States), and the spread of Christianity in foreign parts."[11] Thus the surnames in *Dom Casmurro* indicate the proud blood—the red blood—that courses through the veins of the characters; the saints' names, the influence of a long Christian-Catholic tradition. As the navigators carried the faith with them, so the two elements are wedded in a single character, but—like body and soul—they are essentially incompatible and engender conflict. In some instances the blood has thinned, or has been altered by an admixture of the African; frequently the Christian faith has become a meaningless habit, a veneer, a fad, or a purposeful hypocrisy.

In Uncle Cosme, for example, there had been a considerable thinning of the glorious Portuguese blood: one show of red corpuscles in youth when he was "a devil with the women and a hot-headed party-man," and then, as Santiago puts it, "he lost all ardor," and sank into the role of a lazy, undistinguished colonial. The saint for whom he was named was a Christian martyr, but Uncle Cosme's faith was as pale as his blood. He did not hold with his sister's extreme devotion, mildly suggesting that her promise to God had been made so long ago there was not much point in keeping it, especially if it was going to make her unhappy—or if she wanted to keep it and be unhappy, that was all right too: "God knows what's best for everyone." In other words, "Just don't disturb me." God, to him, was a convenient habit that protected his comfort (much as did his habit of riding to the court-room on a gentle nag) and removed the necessity of pondering right and wrong. For the name "Cosme" ("Cosmo") is related to the Greek "cosmos" ("world"). Uncle Cosme had succumbed to the fleshpots of this world: eating, drinking, backgammon, cursing the clergy, his armchair, and a quiet joke. Capitú called him a *boa vida*—that is, a person who habitually follows the course that will least interfere with his personal comfort. Perhaps a definite cue to the significance of Cosme's name is to be found in the description of his difficulty in mounting his horse each morning. When his uncle finally succeeded in hoisting his fleshy body into the saddle (Santiago tells us), "it was seldom that the mount failed to show by a gesture that she had just received the *world*."

There was that other Cosme ("A Mágoa do Infeliz Cosme"), who was also fond of good living. Though he indulged in a public display of grief over the death of his wife, it did not interfere with his appetite nor prevent him, as we have seen, from selling her jewels, and at a good price.

It is to be noted that Santiago was in some respects a true nephew of Uncle Cosme. When Capitú could not eat the *cocada* because of concern for the future of their love, Santiago ate two—hers and his. After learning of the death of Ezekiel, Santiago "ate a good dinner." When all his family and most of his friends had passed away and he was left with his remorse over the failure of his life, he continued to "eat well and sleep well."

If Uncle Cosme's blood had paled and his faith worn thin, the same cannot be said of his sister. The blood of the conquerors was still strong in Dona Gloria—she was a slave mistress. The livelong day she walked back and forth over the whole house supervising her slaves' work; she sent other slaves into the streets to earn her money; she bought and sold slaves. Her mother before her (not her father, be it noted) and her grandmother had been plantation mistresses. They were hardy pioneer stock of São Paulo. There is possibly an allusion in her surname to Barbara Fernandes, the heroine of Dio, for Dona Gloria was a dynamic woman. Not only did she run her establishment of slaves; she ran her family and other dependents in the same smooth style. And not only was her business ability evinced in her slaving; she invested in stock and real estate; she lent money to Escobar, but kept a wary eye on it; she kept José Dias satisfied with a few coppers; she had a relative for a companion because, it is intimated, she did not have to pay her.

But we see all these qualities, as it were, in the light of a church candle. To her family and dependents she was a "saint." To José Dias she was "Santíssima," and "Santíssima" is the epithet of the Virgin Mary. Her name, "Maria da Gloria," is the name of the Virgin, alluding to her graces and titles. The common noun "glória" is the term used to designate the effulgence surrounding the figures of God, the Holy Ghost, Christ, and Mary in paintings. Certainly the name of God was constantly on Dona Gloria's lips, but what of her pious acts? We have seen that her religious faith did not interfere with her usury. Neither did love of her son prevent her from forcing him into the priesthood against his wish, because, as she herself said, she was afraid God would punish her for breaking her oath. Later when she came to identify herself with Capitú and wished to give Bento to her, as to a part of herself, she swindled God, through a casuistical trick, out of His promised reward. Maria da Gloria Fernandes, like the silk-clad image of Nossa Senhora da Gloria in the near-by church, was a fine, rich, Christian Brazilian lady, but solid oak underneath.

As one would expect, Santiago's names are replete with meaning: "Bento"; the surnames "Fernandes," "Santiago," and "Albuquerque"; even the epithet "Casmurro" has a triple implication.

"Bento" is the usual Portuguese form of "Benedict." St. Benedict and St. Anthony were the saints of the Portuguese people—models of old-fashioned simplicity. In criticizing the clergy of the time, Machado de Assis wrote, "St. Benedict and St. Anthony never dreamed of owning plantations and slaves."[12] (It is to be noted that, in Machado's little gem "Entre Santos," St. Benedict and St. Anthony are absent from the company of sophisticated saints who descend from their altars to discuss their parishoners.) In the same manner, the name "Bento" is applied by Machado de Assis to prosaic, simple souls: for example, there is Bento Facundes da Purificação, the good, hardworking, thrifty druggist of "Dívida Extinta." There is the gullible Bento Soares of "Sem Olhos," "who was profoundly convinced that the whole world has as its boundaries those of the district in which he lived, and that the human species made its appearance on earth the first day of April, 1832, the date of his birth." And there is Bento, the father of Braz Cubas, who was certainly a kindly, simple soul, and, though rich, his humble origin is more than hinted at.[13] We might include the Benedict (the longer form of "Bento") of "Evolução," in whom Machado stressed the prosaic element: " 'What's in a name?' . . . The rose, whatever it is called has the same smell. Let us go to the smell of Benedict. We must agree at once that he was of all men the least Romeo in this world . . ." The same might be said of Bento Santiago: he was the least Romeo in this world. He scarcely knew the difference between the sexes; he was an inch or so shorter than his Juliet; he ate cakes while she did the worrying over their love.

So much for the proper noun. What of the common adjective "bento"? It means "blessed, consecrated to a cult by means of a religious ceremony, favored by Fortune, prosperous, wealthy." All these meanings apply to Bento Santiago. He was blessed by God—in fact his birth was a "miracle." His mother had consecrated him to the Church before his birth. He was wealthy by inheritance, and he made money by his profession. Fortune favored his material circumstances, his love, and his marriage.

There is perhaps still another connotation. A number of saints bear the name "Bento": one of them was a Negro known as St. Benedict the Moor.

It is possible too that the diminutive "Bentinho," by

which he was known at home, has a special, ironic flavor. The common noun "bentinho" denotes a scapular consisting of two pieces of blessed cloth on which prayers are printed. We know what store Bentinho set by prayers, and how he promised them by the hundreds and thousands. We know how he would have left the solution of his problems to God, or to His earthly representative the Emperor Dom Pedro II.

His surnames indicate that there was another side to Bento. Who was this Albuquerque whose blood flowed in our hero's veins? He was, no doubt, the great and famous Dom Afonso de Albuquerque, who founded the Portuguese empire in India and served in Africa and Italy against the Turks. (Particularly, in 1480 he went to help the King of Naples against the Turks.) Camões called him "Albuquerque the Terrible,"[14] and this has been his epithet ever since. Apparently he had a fascination for Machado de Assis. In some reading notes on João de Barros, Machado left a portrait of him, which ends as follows: "He was a little hasty in his executions and did not show much pity, he made himself feared by the Moors and took great precautions to always get the best of them."[15]

When Afonso de Albuquerque died, his body was shrouded in the mantle of the Military Order of Santiago, or as it was formerly written, Sant-Iago—that is, Saint James. "Santiago" was the battle cry of the early Spaniards and Portuguese because, as Camões tells us, this saint was the one who particularly helped in the slaughtering of the Moors.[16] And João de Barros writes that Afonso de Albuquerque had "particular devotion" for the "Apostle Sant-Iago."[17]

Though there were several famous Fernandeses in the Age of Discovery, for Santiago's third family name —considering its close conjunction with the name Albuquerque—one is tempted to believe that Machado had in mind Antonio Fernandes, the Negro cup-bearer and majordomo of Afonso de Albuquerque—a great warrior too and deep in Albuquerque's confidence, but who was, none the less, burned at the stake by order of his master. (What was Machado's note on Albuquerque?—"a little hasty in his executions.") This would mean that Bento's mother and grandmother had Negro blood—perhaps a touch of Machadean irony, but in line with his belief that slavery was not a race question.[18] It would also be a realistic touch, for the first Brazilian colonists brought no women with them and had children by their Negro slaves.[19]

Now, let us take another look at these three surnames. I do not recall that Machado de Assis ever referred to Albuquerque by his common epithet of "Terrible," though he was of course familiar with it. But he does use this epithet in two different stories, and both times for the same personage—Shakespeare's Othello.[20] He also applies the term "terrible" twice within three sentences to the jealous husband of "Sem Olhos"—the husband of whom the narrator says: "What other rival of Othello is there to compare with this husband who burned out with a blazing brand the most beautiful eyes in the world in punishment for their having *looked* at another pair of eyes?"

Notice the other similarities between Albuquerque and Othello. Othello helped Venice in its fight against the Turks; Albuquerque helped Naples fight the Turks. Albuquerque was hasty in his executions, so was Othello. That there may be no doubt of the Negroid blood in *our* Albuquerque, we have the "dusky" "thicklips," Fernandes, and perhaps also St. Benedict the Moor. And like Othello, he too was descended "from men of royal siege."

To return to the name Santiago: it, like the other two surnames, was a good old Portuguese Discovery name. But let us examine it from a linguistic point of view. Santiago tells us that he had a "married couple" inside him, each consort struggling for the upper hand—a good angel and a bad. (Though he would identify the good element with his mother, the bad with Capitú, there is reason to believe, as we shall see, that he was confused.) A number of Shakespearean critics have gathered evidence to show that *Othello* is a miracle play, with Desdemona representing Christ and Iago the devil in a struggle for Othello's soul.[21] Other critics, as already remarked, though not going along with the miracle-play idea, still believe that Desdemona symbolizes the good in Othello, Iago the evil. The name "Santiago" fits neatly into a similar construction in our hero: he is part saint (Sant'), part Iago—the good or saintly and the Iago qualities at war with each other for his soul. A comparable duality is represented by contrary connotations in the names "Bento" and "Albuquerque." As if further to point up this heaven-and-earth struggle, Machado de Assis gave one of his hero's names to two schoolmates who typify his two conflicting, unfulfilled hopes—one to make a success in the world, and the other to lay up treasure in heaven. These were the Albuquerque brothers, "one of whom is a canon in Bahia, while the other went into medicine and, they say, has discovered a specific against yellow fever."[22]

There is a pun in the nickname "Casmurro," I believe, which clinches all this word play, but that will be discussed in a more appropriate place.

When we turn to the other members of Dona Gloria's household, we are fortunate in finding among them one with a name of the Oliveira type—that is, a name Machado used again and again to signify a certain trait of character, or rather a composite of traits. This is the name "José" ("Joseph"), which he conferred upon no less than twenty-three important characters appearing in various novels and tales,[23] and on a fictional character that turns up spasmodically in his journalistic columns.[24]

A comparison of these fictional Josés makes it clear that the traits typified by this name are those of an ordinary, conventional man, with his feet on the ground, a man of limited learning and limited imagination, an officious, wordy man, given to voicing the obvious or what generally passes for true. He is often a servant, or with a servile way about him, and frequently hypocritical. Some of the Josés are all José, and José is all there is; in other instances José is only one phase of the person, who has other—perhaps more important—traits suggested by his surnames. Machado de Assis thus describes one of his early Josés: "He was average in everything except in his intellect—which was of the lowest order."[25] That is, he was basically *José*. On the other hand, Agostinho José dos Santos of *Esaú e Jacob* (note the other names), though vulgar, practical (he was a successful banker), and conventional, was not stupid in most respects, and he had a rather extravagant imagination—believing, as a Spiritualist, that he was the father of two reincarnated Apostles. Even so, the practical and mundane predominated, for he did not have "five minutes to spend in evoking his late teacher of Spiritualism because he had some lucrative liquidations to take care of."[26]

Sr. José Brito was the nemesis of the playboy Vasconcellos ("O Segrêdo de Augusta")—the nemesis of "reality" in the form of bookkeeping, interest, bills, foreclosures, and the voicing of homely, unpleasant truths. He was a creditor.

One of the most thoroughgoing Josés, and one who discloses his nature in all its unspoiled simplicity, is José Rodrigues, the imaginary servant to the columnist Machado de Assis. He seems to represent a homely strain in the sophisticated columnist—his stupid, prosaic side, the man in the street as opposed to the poet-philosopher in the ivory tower, the body to the soul, Sancho Panza to Don Quixote—and there is often a strain of practical wisdom in his rambling conversations.

Seven other of Machado's Josés are servants or are employed in a servile capacity in a wealthy house. One of these, Ayres's servant, who, along with his master, appears in both *Esaú e Jacob* and *Memorial de Ayres*,[27] poses an interesting question. Why, in these two final novels, did Machado de Assis give the name "José" to both master and servant? But Ayres was the servant of his country, with no soul he could call his own, moved like a pawn all over the world, all acts of free will subordinated to his career. As he said of himself, "I was born to serve."[28] The diplomacy of the master—the "always having the right remark for the right occasion," the concealing of his own thoughts—is reflected in the servant's flattery, lying, and petty thievery. The master's propensity for prying into the lives of others, because he had no life of his own, is matched by the servant's poking his nose into his master's business. The servant's hypocritical, perfunctory religion finds its counterpart in Ayres, who "said an ode of Horace," instead of a prayer, before falling asleep. The officiousness of the servant and his ignorance are lacking in Ayres—but then he had some other names: "Costa," "Marcondes," and "Ayres." In *Esaú e Jacob*, of course, there is the third José—Agostinho José dos Santos. Why this plethora of Josephs? It is, I believe, a comment on the society Machado de Assis was satirizing in this novel.

Perhaps Machado's Josés contain an allusion to the Joseph of the Old Testament, who was sold into slavery by his brothers and who finally ingratiated himself with the Pharaoh by giving excellent, if not miraculous, advice—much as José Dias ingratiated himself with Santiago's father and mother with *his* advice and miraculous cure of their slaves. Apparently, also, "José" was a common name for slaves in Brazil at the time in which the early scenes of *Dom Casmurro* take place.[29] Whatever the reason behind the name, the class of characters designated by it would seem fairly well defined. It is no less clear that José Dias fits into this class, is perhaps its crowning glory—the embodiment of all that is José-esque in superlative degree, for

46

superlativeness was his great claim to individuality.

The surname "Dias" is a good old Portuguese name, borne, notably, by Bartolomeu Dias, the first man to round the Cape of Good Hope, in 1488—and José Dias, one recalls, was fond of travel. The common noun "dia" means "day," and the Dias coat of arms bears a golden sun on a field of blue. But the name "Dias" is also as common in Portuguese as "Smith" in English: possibly Machado de Assis wanted to accentuate José Dias's vulgarity.

In a sense, José Dias sums up and symbolizes the mediocrity and superficiality of Dona Gloria and her circle. But there is another side to José Dias which sets him apart from the rest of Machado's Josés.[30] His saint was the father of the Holy Family. St. Joseph is not only regarded as patron saint of the family and prayed to for assistance in household and family problems; he is also the protector of the Church Temporal and the patron of the Beautiful Death, because he himself had the most beautiful death possible in having Christ present with him. José Dias's function as protector of the Santiago family is obvious; even his relation to the "Santíssima" Dona Gloria and Bentinho resembles St. Joseph's respectful, protective role toward the Virgin and Christ Child. His protective attitude toward the Brazilian Church, and indeed toward the Pope himself—that is, toward the Church Temporal —is frequently displayed. But it is St. Joseph's tribute as patron of the Beautiful Death which is most conclusively attached to José Dias; it confirms not only his own role in the Santiago family but also that of Gloria as Virgin Mary and Bento as the Christ.

When José Dias died, Santiago was at his bedside.
José Dias's last superlative . . . [was] the best of them all, the sweetest, one which made death a fragment of life . . .
He died serene, after a short agony. A little

while before, he had heard us say the sky was beautiful and had asked us to open the window . . .

We opened the window. As a matter of fact, the sky was blue and clear. José Dias raised his head and gazed out. After a few seconds he fell back murmuring, "*Most beautiful!*" They were the last words he uttered in this world.

"Sun" and "blue sky," in Machado de Assis's vocabulary, designate "pure love" and "innocent trust,"[31] so that both José Dias's death and his family coat of arms associate him with the Christ. And "rounding the Cape of Good Hope" was used elsewhere by Machado as a symbol for conquering lust and selfishness.[32]

Among the names of the Padua family one finds nothing redolent of old Portuguese heroes, and even the Christian element is overshadowed by other, more powerful suggestions. "Padua" is a common Portuguese name, but a humble name supposed to derive from St. Anthony of Padua. Our Padua's Christian name "João," like its English equivalent "John," is also one of the commonest of given names—and we know Padua was a common kind of fellow, a vulgar man who liked rough company, according to José Dias, and certainly a simple man. But to Machado de Assis, as to us, the name "Padua" no doubt called to mind "Signior Benedick of Padua," "Signior Baptista a gentleman of Padua," the law-clerk Portia "new come from Padua." Padua is a little city thirty-five kilometers from Venice, identified by Machado de Assis *with* Venice.[33] Venice in Machado de Assis frequently stands for Rio de Janeiro, and the Venetian Republic, the "Seteníssima República," for Brazil.[34] Certainly João Padua was one of the weak-headed Brazilian men governed by his superior womenfolk such as Machado often portrayed. I believe Machado de Assis wished to give him a Shakespearean flavor with the name, recalling at once Baptista, the father of Katharine the shrew, and Braban-

48

tio, the father of Desdemona—both of whom were helpless in the hands of their daughters. Capitú ruled her
father, though more subtly and gently than did Katharine, and deceived him, as Desdemona did Brabantio.
Indeed, Machado de Assis used the name "Baptista"
to designate Shakespearean types: in *Resurreição* for
an "Iago"; in *Esaú e Jacob* for a man cursed with two
shrews at home—his wife, a political-minded lady
likened by Machado to Lady Macbeth, and a beautiful
daughter in revolt against her parents, who did not
understand her, as in the case of Shakespeare's Baptista and Katharine. Like Brabantio, our Padua was a
government official, as has already been mentioned;
and, though not a "magnifico," he did get to carry the
pole of the canopy once in a procession of the Blessed
Sacrament.[35]

Any deep significance in the name of Capitú's mother
has so far eluded me. (The legend of St. Fortunata
seems to yield nothing pertinent.) "Fortunata" is a
Latin adjective meaning "blessed by fortune, lucky."
Of course, Fortunata's husband won a grand prize in
the lottery, which *she* spent in a provident manner;
she had a happy home life, and saw her daughter well
married. In addition to her providential manner of
governing her husband, her habit of briefly appearing
during the love-making scenes between Bento and
Capitú gives the feeling that she may be intended to
represent the goddess Fortuna—slightly irresponsible
as that goddess is often represented—smiling on their
love. Her name might point to Madeira or the Ca-
nary Islands—together anciently known as Fortunatae
Insulae—as the place of her origin; that theory, whatever else it connotes, would connect her with her husband's songbirds.

Capitú's name, "Capitolina," also has a Roman ring.
It seems to have been used only this once by Machado
de Assis, though he frequently employed the noun
"capitólio" ("Capitolium" and "Capitol"), from which

it derives. In Portuguese this noun is primarily used in a figurative sense as a common noun meaning "triumph, glory, eminence, splendor, magnificence." Machado used this word in the above meanings, and also in the more specialized sense to be found in the saying "Do capitólio à rocha Tarpeia não vai mais que um passo," in which it signifies "the glories or pleasures of this world" as well as "the glories of a high position." In Capitú's name, it is likely that Machado intended all the above denotations, as witness her queenly beauty and dignity, her fondness for dress, her ambition both intellectual and social, shown in her desire to learn Latin, English, lace making, painting, piano, and singing, in her interest in the coronation festivities, and in her admiration for Julius Caesar, "a man who could do everything." Her ability to enjoy the pleasures of this world is shown in the naturalness with which she engaged in the love making and deceived her parents, in her enjoyment of simple fun: "Capitú loved fun and amusement."[36] In other words, her unrepressed, human qualities are symbolized by a pagan name, just as Bento's inhibitions are symbolized by a name loaded with Christian implications. But, I believe, the name "Capitolina" has a special connotation. As pointed out above, the heroine of *Resurreição*, Livia, seems to be Capitú in embryo, as its hero Felix (whose name means "blessed by the gods") contains the embryo of Bento ("blessed by God").

In Livia, Machado portrayed a proud, intelligent, but generous and loving, woman. Livia is not a saint's name. On the contrary, one immediately thinks of Livia the wife of the Emperor Augustus, who was identified with the Roman Capitolium. When Livia first appears in the novel her young friend Rachel calls her "the queen of the evening," and the author comments, "indeed Livia did have the air of a queen, a natural majesty, not a conventional and affected formality but a grandeur that was involuntary and her own."[37]

The Empress Livia was given the title "Augusta." We know beyond any possibility of doubt that Machado de Assis associated queenly dignity and the warmth of a generous love with the name "Augusta." At the end of the short story "Qual dos Dois?" he upbraids the heroine Augusta for not living up to her name, or rather for exaggerating and perverting her Augusta-like quality of pride into a heartless and despotic vanity.

> Repelling those who loved her, frivolous and inconstant in her actions, endowed with a proud and haughty spirit, Augusta reaped the reward of her own mistakes . . .

> No one should imitate Augusta, she is one of those rare, exaggerated types who can never be a loving wife nor a devoted mother; in short, she is a woman without one trace of *augusta*.

But the name, perhaps, hits closer home. Machado's wife was named "Carolina Augusta." In one of his two (published) love letters to her, he speaks of her "imperium" over him (that is, her right to command); this is the same word used of Capitú.[38] And further on in the letter, he writes:

> Mind and heart like yours are rare gifts; a soul so good and noble, a sensibility so delicate, reason so straight and true, are not treasures that nature scatters generously among the members of your sex. You belong to the very small number of women who . . . have the ability to both love and feel, and think.[39]

The novel *Resurreição* was sold to B. L. Garnier in a contract dated September 30, 1869, with delivery promised "the middle of November of the current year."[40] In that same month Machado married his Carolina Augusta.[41] It is perhaps not surprising that

51

the Livia (Augusta) of *Resurreição* combines queenly manner and intellect with generosity of soul and loving warmth, or that Machado de Assis continued to associate these qualities with the name "Augusta" and even with her home, the Capitolium. This Carolina Augusta was no passing fancy: their marriage lasted thirty-five years, ending only with Carolina's death. For the remaining four years of his life Machado de Assis's letters to his friends are filled with his grief, and he wrote a last novel in which there are three heroines—all Carolina Augusta.[42]

As if to call our attention to the significance of Bento's and Capitú's names, the confession of their love begins with Capitú joining their names on the garden wall.

> I read our two names [writes Santiago], carved with a nail and disposed thus:
>
> BENTO
> CAPITOLINA

It was the beginning of their love. In a deeper sense it was the whole story—the conflict of two natures.

Two other points are to be noted about this inscription. Through it we first learn Capitú's true name, so that it becomes doubly significant—a dramatic drawing aside of a curtain. Secondly, the names appear in the book in large Roman capitals. Machado de Assis was in the habit of specifying the size and kind of type to be used for quotations. He seems to have been even rather fussy in these matters.[43]

One further detail of Capitú's name may be important. In the Saints' Legend, the Cappadocian lady Capitolina was accompanied in her martydom by her handmaiden Erotheis (sometimes written "Erotis" or "Erotes"). "Erotheis" is apparently connected with the Greek root "erot-" meaning "love" (as seen for example in "Eros" and "Erotes")—a meaning that would not be lost on Machado de Assis, whose interest in the classics is evinced by constant allusion in his writings. Indeed, in later life, he took up the study of the ancient Greek language.[44] St. Capitolina and her handmaiden St. "Love" were martyred A.D. 304.

The names of the other connections of the Santiago house, though perhaps not so closely related to the plot, contribute their bit; and they are in any case appropriate to their bearers. To begin with a lesser one, Dr. João da Costa, the family doctor. "Costa" is a good old Portuguese Discovery name. But the basic meaning of the common noun "costa" is "rib," and the escutcheon of the Costa family has six silver ribs in two pales on a field of red topped by a crest of two crossed ribs. In other words, Machado named him Dr. Rib much as he might have named him Dr. Clavicle or Dr. Shinbone—to belittle his professional ability. Santiago, one recalls, sums up his "therapeutics" in two words—"leeches and emetics"—and intimates that his main excellence was as an extra hand at *voltarete.* Note too the given name "João," the same as Padua's, to further drive home the insignificance of the man. One must admit, the minds of Dona Gloria's circle were not of the first water.

Padre Cabral's name has a truly glorious ring. There was, for example, Pedro Álvares Cabral, companion of Afonso de Albuquerque and reputed discoverer of Brazil. There was another Cabral, not quite so famous, but more nearly resembling our Padre—Brother Manuel Cabral, eminent Latinist and writer of the eighteenth century. The verger called Padre Cabral "model padre," "good Latinist," but Santiago hints that he did not learn much Latin from him.[45] There are indications that, as with Dr. João da Costa, Padre Cabral was at his best at the gaming table. ("'He had a way with dice,' gently sighed the verger, 'the throw of a master.'")[46] And Santiago tells us he was something of a gourmet—a nice companion piece to Uncle Cosme—a commodious father confessor to a commodious colonial! The blood had thinned.

Cousin Justina's name is self-explanatory (though, curiously enough, St. Justina was a virgin martyr of Padua): she was just, especially in her speech. She always gave the devil his due—in the strict if not the usual sense of the word. To quote Santiago: "She said frankly to Peter the evil she thought of Paul, and to Paul what she thought of Peter."[47] In short, she never spoke better of a person than the person deserved.

If Cousin Justina did not exert an influence on Santiago, at least she reflects an ungenerous element in his character: a tendency to look for the worst in people and suspect their motives.

Escobar's name—Ezekiel de Souza Escobar—not only indicates his character but also ties in directly to the plot. Santiago, in discussing his son, explains the origin and meaning of the name "Ezekiel" by two quotations from the Old Testament: "Thou wast perfect in thy ways from the day that thou was created," and "Ezekiel son of man." The two quotations have the same meaning, for "son of man" means man in his perfect, simple state as he came from the hand of God —in contrast to the perverted men whom the prophet Ezekiel tried to convert to their pristine ways of purity. Though Santiago put his own construction on these two quotations in an attempt to persuade the reader of his son's illegitimacy, there seems no reason why, for Escobar at least, we should not take them at their face value. They bear out Santiago's portrait of Escobar, if we leave to one side the former's jealous suspicions. Escobar was a fine specimen of the human race: physically strong and handsome, endowed with rare intellectual gifts, kind, and generous. If we consider the New Testament, an aura of divinity is added to both Escobar and Ezekiel: Jesus refers to himself as Son of man (for example, Mark 9:9); and the angels at His tomb call Him Son of man (Luke 24:7).

"Souza" and "Escobar" were names prominent in the Age of Discovery. Martim Afonso de Souza, one of the

54

most illustrious of the Portuguese warriors and navigators, is responsible for the name "Rio de Janeiro," which he applied to the bay. Thomé de Souza was the first governor of Brazil; a Lopes de Souza was the first *capitão* of the province in which our Escobar was born. There was a high-born navigator, Pero Escobar, who piloted one of the four ships in Vasco de Gama's discovery of the sea route to India: he is described by João de Barros. It may be recalled that Santiago, in describing the close friendship between himself and Escobar, quoted a long passage from João de Barros's work.[48] But we must remember that it was Machado de Assis, not Santiago, who gave Escobar his name. And there was another Escobar with whom Machado de Assis was still more familiar—the famous Jesuit casuist of that name whom Pascal attacked in his *Provinciales.*[49] Ezekiel Escobar was the author of the casuistical device by which Santiago was freed from the seminary: Dona Gloria paid for the education to the priesthood of a poor orphan—that is, substituted a scapegoat for the promised sacrifice of her son to God. And there are other indications of Jesuitical reasoning powers on the part of Escobar: for example, the finesse of the argument for spelling reform; his observation to the effect that one may best serve God out in the world; and his remark in respect to his and Santiago's quitting the seminary, "Once more religion and liberty become boon companions."[50] In this last bit of logic the Jesuit and the navigator join hands; but it is nevertheless the watchword of Escobar's life. As Uncle Cosme used his religious faith to further soften a soft life, Escobar accommodated his to the needs of an aggressive life in the marts of trade. The meaning of the Hebrew word "Ezekiel" is "whom God strengthens."

Though Santiago's son was named, strictly speaking, not by Machado de Assis but by Santiago himself, there are two interesting details concerning *his* name. The prophet Ezekiel, who, in the Catholic tradition, is also a saint and a martyr because he was killed by a Jewish judge turned pagan, was buried in Babylon in the tomb of Shem. Ezekiel Santiago was buried, with a good deal of ceremony, "in the vicinity of Jerusalem." Santiago evidently knew the exact location but does not pass the information on to the reader. The second detail of Ezekiel's name has more point. Santiago's father was Pedro de Albuquerque Santiago. We are not informed of Bento Santiago's full name but we do know that friends and acquaintances called him "Santiago." When Ezekiel returned home as a young man, he sent in his card, which read

EZEKIEL A. de SANTIAGO

That is, he had reduced the ancestral "Albuquerque" to an initial, and of necessity the "de" was transferred to the position before "Santiago"; but, thus, the genitive "de Santiago" becomes a patronymic, "son of Santiago"—as though it were being stated that Ezekiel was in fact Santiago's son. As with Bento's and Capitú's names on the wall, the name on the calling card appears in the printed book in large Roman capitals—a detail, we can rest assured, seen to by Machado de Assis.[51]

The names of Capitú's friend Sancha and her father Gurgel do not afford much of a handle to their meaning. The only things Sancha Gurgel had in common with the Portuguese princess who became a saint were her gentle, submissive nature and her early retirement to a nunlike life. But there is a Spanish saying, also current in Portugal, with many variants,

> Pecadora de Sancha!
> quería y no tenía blanca!

> Pecadora de Sancha!
> quería beber y
> no tenía blanca!
>   etc.

which means "Sancha had the desire but no means of satisfying it." Santiago conveys the impression that Sancha was "interested" in him, and his quotation from Dante in this regard is pretty strong for a mild interest,[52] but he also makes it clear that there was really nothing between them.

The name "Gurgel" (also spelled "Gorgel"), of honorable origin and borne notably by the defender of Rio de Janeiro against the French, Bento Gurgel, resembles the common noun "gorgel" or "gorjal" ("gorget"), which comes from "gorja" ("gullet"). There is another word which by sound and sense reminds one of Sancha's father—"Gorjala," the name of a gluttonous giant in Brazilian folklore. Santiago informs us that Gurgel inclined to a big stomach and had a coarse face. But there are derivatives from "gorja" indicating the other function of the throat: "gorgeia" ("trilling"), "gorjeador" ("a babbler"). Sancha's father was something of a talker.[53] Indeed, his main function in relation to the plot is to serve as a kind of oracle— an oracle which Santiago repudiated. It was Gurgel who pointed out the resemblance between Capitú and the portrait of Sancha's mother, and uttered the Delphic line, "In life there are these strange resemblances."

If the meanings here are a bit tenuous, the more obvious signification in the remaining two names, "Marcolini" and "Manduca," will amply make up for the difficulty of Sancha's and Gurgel's, and reassure us as to the important role of the names in *Dom Casmurro*.[54]

Marcolini, as befits an opera singer, has an Italian name. Not only that, it was a name borne by a famous singer, Marietta Marcolini, of a generation or so before Machado de Assis, for whom Rossini composed some of his operas. But let us examine "Marcolini" for a Portuguese content. As was true of Custódio Marques, whose name was discussed above, there seems to be a trace of the verb "marcar," in its sense of "to mark out," as, "to mark out" an itinerary, a destiny, or the pattern of a dance. Santiago refers to the chapters on Marcolini and his lengthy comparison of life to an opera as a digression. But is it? It is true that Marcolini appears but once, and only to explain his theory of life. But he is, rather, a prologue "marking out" in symbolic form the story to come, the struggle within Santiago between good and evil, spirituality and sensuality, love and self-love—which is the plot.

The episode of Santiago and the leper boy, and their polemic over the far-away struggle between Russia and Turkey, has also been classed as a digression by some. But again, the boy's name alone forces us to the conclusion that this passage is integral to the unfolding of the struggle within Santiago. For with the story of Manduca, Machado de Assis puts his finger on the weak spot in Santiago's nature—the weakness which caused his downfall.

"Manduca" is a Brazilian term of endearment given those named Manuel.[55] And we are shown the love, care, and consideration lavished on this boy by his poor parents. This name may also connote his disease: the verb "manducar" is a coarse term for the verb "comer" ("eat"), and we are told that the "disease was eating away part of his flesh." But it is the boy's correct name which is most significant.

The name "Manuel" will no doubt suggest the most famous of Manuels, the fourteenth king of Portugal, Manuel the Fortunate, in whose reign occurred the greatest events of Portuguese history: Vasco de Gama's discovery of the sea route to India; the discovery of Brazil by Cabral, and Labrador by the Corte-Reals; the great conquests of Albuquerque at Ormuz, Goa, and Malaca; Magellan's circumnavigation of the globe —the king whose very name is synonymous with the wealth of India, the king in whose reign men *lived* their hopes and dreams. It would seem like a cruel irony on Machado's part to name this poor leper boy after Manuel the Fortunate—but is it? Manduca, it would seem, had nothing—worse than nothing—for he was cursed with a cruel disease. He had received none of the blessings from life that Santiago had. Santiago names those blessings—health, wealth, social standing, friends. But he had the one thing Santiago lacked—a great capacity for love: love of, and faith in, a man, a people, a cause, life. From his dark, fetid sickroom he wrote Bento his impassioned arguments for Turkey, his love and passion for life, his *faith*— "the first, like the last, like all of them ended with the same eternal prediction: 'The Russians will not enter Constantinople!'"

For a brief time he encompassed Santiago with his love and faith, with his love of life. And for a time Santiago's soul bloomed in the radiance cast by Manduca. "Nature beckoned to Manduca with a flower [says Santiago] and perhaps the flower thus took on beauty." We know from the chapter on Bento's sonnet ("O flower of Heaven! O flower bright and pure!") that Santiago identified himself or his soul with a "flower," so that Santiago's statement "Nature beckoned to Manduca with a flower and perhaps the flower thus took on beauty" means in plain language: some better instinct in Santiago, or, as he calls it in the preceding chapter, "an unintentional virtue,"[56] prompted him to take part in the argument with Manduca; in the process some of the beauty of Manduca's soul rubbed off on the flower Santiago. Finally the bloom died away and left only a faint odor of self-love: he had this consolation, that he had given "two or three months of happiness to a poor devil."[57] But Santiago was mistaken. Manduca was not a "poor devil"; he was Manuel the Fortunate, who possessed the wealth of India. Santiago was the poor devil. He had *everything*, yet he did not know how to love; and he had no faith.

His heart was a frail bark driven from its course by every gust; he was nephew of Uncle Cosme, who had "lost all ardor, public and private"; he was a kinsman of Felix, whose heart, if it rose from the dead, soon sank back into the tomb. Or, as Santiago said of himself, he did not succeed in destroying the sloth which his soul had brought from the cradle and life had not lessened.[58]

It is noteworthy that Manduca had only a given name, like a king or a god. Indeed, his name connotes more than Manuel the Fortunate. "Manuel" is a shortened form of "Emmanuel"—"Immanuel" in English—the Biblical word from the Hebrew meaning "God is with us" or "God is within us." It is the term Isaiah used for the prophesied Messiah: "Behold a virgin shall conceive, and bear a son, and shall call his name *Immanuel.*" In Matthew (1:23) the prophecy of Isaiah is applied to the miraculous birth of Jesus from the Virgin Mary. Thus, in the Catholic countries the name "Manuel" has been applied to Christ,[59] in particular, in relation to the transubstantiation in the Blessed Sacrament, whereby the communicant literally —even physically—places "God within" him by drinking the wine and eating the bread. As a matter of fact, King Manuel the Fortunate was named "Manuel" because he was born on Corpus Christi, the feast day commemorating the institution of the Blessed Sacrament.[60] Even the pet-name "Manduca" points to this interpretation of "Manuel."

> Qui *manducat* meam carnem, et bibit meum sanguinem habet vitam aeternam . . .
> qui *manducat* meam carnem, et bibit meum sanguinem, in me manet et ego in illo [John 6:55 and 6:57].[61]

In Manduca, Machado de Assis equated love, life, and the spirit of Jesus Christ: "I am the resurrection and the life." It will be recalled that when Santiago pauses in his writing of the Manduca story, he looks out the window and sees another boy named Manduca, who "is not a leper" and is "flying a kite." That even the inattentive reader may not escape the implication, he not only comments on this other Manduca's name but makes this further observation: "Everything out here *breathes life*." Apparently Santiago is not conscious of the import of his own words, for again he has his signals reversed. He titles the final chapter of the Manduca episode "The devil is not so black as he is painted," and he goes to some pains to convey the impression that the devil is represented in Manduca. But of course the devil is in Santiago, and what Santiago calls the devil is God, so that the title might better have been: "Great is the mystery of godliness: God was manifest in the flesh [1 Timothy 3:16]"— or, as Machado de Assis wrote elsewhere, "God writes straight with crooked lines."[62]

5

Santiago's Disease

WITH THE DEATH of Manduca a shadow falls across the idyll of Bento and Capitú. Santiago tells us that as he left the dead boy's house his golden thoughts of love lost their luster and their metal turned to ashes. It is a foretoken of the bigger shadow that was to envelop the love in Santiago's heart and kill it. He himself felt the chilling force, and grasped desperately at physical love. Just as in the chapter on the "Combing of the braids," when he felt his own inadequacy before Capitú's stronger emotion, felt himself slipping into the vast tide of love in her eyes, and grasped her hair with his "physical" hands; so, now, after seeing the dead Manduca, his thoughts were: "Love, lads! and, above all, love beautiful, spirited girls. They have a remedy for ills, fragrance to sweeten a stench; for death they give you life . . . Love, lads, love!"

To continue the parallel implicit in this episode, Manduca was killed by a "horrible disease—leprosy," and "in order to enter the tomb spent three years in dissolution." In Santiago the Manduca quality (capacity for love) was killed by a leprosy of the soul, and was fifteen years in the process of dissolution. Santiago called his disease "jealousy"; and it too ate him, ate away his love, trust, generosity—all his fine qualities. For Santiago had fine qualities; he was toward being a man in the highest sense of the word.

That was why Capitú loved him. That is why we feel the tragedy of his failure.

Let us consider the course of Santiago's "disease," as he recounts it.

The first symptom appeared (he says) when José Dias visited him in the seminary and let fall the careless remark that Capitú was gay and happy as ever and just waiting to "hook" some young dandy of the neighborhood and marry him. The chapter in which this is related is entitled "A touch of Iago." The immediate effect of José Dias's news was to send Santiago into a trance in which he lost consciousness of his surroundings and had a daydream of running wildly to Capitú's house, grabbing her, and forcing the truth out of her. This first attack of jealousy seems entirely justifiable. It is only natural that he should be jealous of the dashing young aristocrats who rode past Capitú's house, with their fine boots and spurs, on their blooded mounts—especially when we recall that he "did not yet know how to ride and was afraid of a horse." But underneath is perhaps a deeper conflict. In this same chapter José Dias had mentioned Dona Gloria's tears, occasioned by her son's absence, and the next two chapters are given over to Santiago's dream that night, with an indication of its meaning: that is, a doubt that he ought to love and marry Capitú rather than become a priest and continue as the loving son of his mother.

The second attack of Santiago's jealousy occurred at the conclusion of Escobar's first visit to the Santiago house. Capitú had had no part in this visit—had not seen Escobar—but when he and Santiago were bidding each other fond farewells in the street, she was looking out at them from her front window. And as Santiago lingered at the door, waiting to see whether Escobar would wave to him from the omnibus, Capitú, at her window, said, "What great friend is this?" Whereupon, Santiago ends his chapter: " 'It was Escobar,' said I. I went and stood beneath her window and looked up."

It is to be noted that here is reproduced the situation of Santiago's dream, described nine chapters earlier, after his first attack of jealousy. In the dream, as Santiago was watching Capitú's window, spying for young dandies, one ran away, and Santiago went up to Capitú.

To return to Santiago's narrative: at the precise moment he took his place under Capitú's window a young dandy rode down the street, stared at Capitú, and continued to stare at her as he rode on. "This," comments Santiago, "was the second fang jealousy sank into me." In other words, he thought he was jealous of the dandy. But to make certain the reader understands the real situation in his soul, Santiago inserts two metaphorical chapters between his reply, "It was Escobar," and the passage of the dandy on horseback.

In the first, entitled "A dramatic reform," he tells us that destiny, like other dramatists, does not announce its sudden reversals of fortune, nor the final catastrophe, they each arrive at their appointed time; that there is room for reform in this method, and he suggests that the drama begin with the end. He then illustrates his proposal with Shakespeare's *Othello*.

The second chapter, entitled "The stage manager," is so necessary to an understanding of Santiago's jealousy that I shall transcribe it almost in full.

> Destiny is not only a dramatist, it is also its own stage manager. That is, it sets the entrances of the characters on scene, gives them letters and other objects, and produces the off-stage noises to go with the dialogue: thunder, a carriage, a shot. When I was young, they performed here, in some theater or other, a drama that ended with the Last Judgment. The principal character was Ahasuerus, who, in the last scene, concluded a monologue with this exclamation, "I hear the

trumpet of the archangel!" No trumpet was heard at all. Ahasuerus, covered with shame, repeated the line, this time louder, to cue the stage manager, but still nothing. Then he walked toward the back, under a pretense of tragic gesture, but actually for the purpose of whispering into the wings, "The cornet! the cornet! the cornet!" The audience caught this word and burst into laughter, so that when the trumpet sounded in earnest and Ahasuerus shouted for the third time that it was that of the archangel, a little urchin in the pit corrected from here below, "No, senhor, it is the archangel's cornet!"

In the same way may be explained my being under Capitú's window and the passage of a man on horseback, a *dandy*, as we used to say in those days. He sat astride a beautiful bay. . . . Others had passed by, and still others would come after; all were on their way to see their sweethearts . . .

Well, the dandy on the bay horse did not pass by like the others: he was the trumpet of doom, and sounded on time. That is the way with destiny, which is its own stage manager. The rider was not content to pass on, but turned his head in our direction, the direction of Capitú, and looked at Capitú . . .

The full interpretation seems to be this: Escobar was the trumpet of doom; the dandy, the cornet. Santiago cued the stage manager with the line: "It was Escobar." And the stage manager destiny sounded "the cornet," that is, "the dandy." The implication both from the dream and these three chapters, is that Escobar was the object of Santiago's jealousy long before Capitú had seen him and before Escobar had seen her, and much earlier still, at the time of the dream when Capitú did not even know of Escobar's existence, nor he of hers. Destiny by sounding "the cornet" "on time" made the dandy seem to be the "trumpet of doom," that is, Santiago's subconscious jealousy of Escobar appeared on the scene as a conscious jealousy of the dandy. But none of this reached Santiago's consciousness at the time—whatever the narrator Santiago makes of it.

One may detect also an element of vanity, or of homosexual jealousy, in the Escobar-dandy sequence. Santiago looked after the omnibus to see if Escobar loved him enough to look back from the distance, "but he did not." Consider the dandy, who now represented Escobar to him: "The horse went on but the man's head continued to stare back" *at Capitú.*

For the next fifteen years Santiago's jealousy appeared as a chronic disturbance, flaring up briefly because of various small local irritations. Cousin Justina aroused it by suggesting that Capitú had stayed at Sancha's because she and Sancha were flirting with young men. On the honeymoon, Capitú seemed to him overly eager to go back to Rio de Janeiro: she must have married him for money and position. Later his jealousy was roused by her dancing partners at balls, by her inattention to his lectures on astronomy, by her contemplation of the sea, by her forgetting of the peddler's song; because their son Ezekiel did not resemble him. His jealousy was roused because he fancied Ezekiel resembled Escobar—but here the real object of Santiago's jealousy was beginning to thrust itself into his conscious mind. The next chapter, "Third party claim proceeding," in which Santiago returned home unexpectedly and found Escobar at the front door, intimates as much. But in this same chapter and in the following but one, Santiago also sums up his conscious jealousy which had continued through the years in spite of the happiness of his marriage:

> [Capitú's] slightest gesture tormented me, a casual word, the urging of a simple request; often indifference alone was enough. I became jealous

66

of everything and everyone. A neighbor, a partner in a waltz, any man young or old filled me with terror and mistrust.

Five brief chapters later, Escobar again began to loom in Santiago's consciousness. When Escobar told him that he had planned "a family project" for the four of them, namely, Santiago, Capitú, Escobar, and Sancha, Santiago asked sarcastically, "For the four of us? A *contradança*?" Now, a contradança is danced with the couples facing each other, that is, Escobar would dance opposite Capitú, Santiago opposite Sancha. But "contradança" also has the figurative meaning of a topsy-turvy state of confusion—in politics at least —of a moral or, rather, immoral mixup. Santiago immediately began to put the contradança suggestion to work by gazing meaningfully into Sancha's eyes and squeezing her hand. In the same chapter, Santiago's envy of Escobar, is openly stated, for when he felt the muscles of Escobar's arms, he says: "I found them thicker and stronger than mine, and I envied them." The figurative meaning of the word contradança is perhaps reflected in Santiago's confusion of Escobar's arms with Sancha's ("I felt his arms as though I were feeling those of Sancha"), and certainly in his perturbation of mind which followed this scene and lasted for several hours.

Four pages later, and only some thirty-odd pages from the end of the novel, the jealousy of Escobar broke completely into Santiago's conscious mind— when he saw Capitú gaze for a moment at Escobar's corpse and wipe away "a few, quiet tears." The remaining chapters relate his half-hearted attempts to thrust the specter back into the subconscious, his detection of evidence of Capitú's unfaithfulness in her every tear and word, in scenes recalled from the past, and in Ezekiel's resemblance to Escobar; and they relate Santiago's revenge.

It is in these final chapters, when Santiago throws off all pretense, that we come to a full realization of how his "disease" has changed him from "Bento" into "Dom Casmurro"; and to a full realization of Santiago's purpose in writing his story.

6

Why Publish?

WHY DID SANTIAGO write his story? Machado de Assis must have intended the reader to ask this question, because his fictitious author anticipates it at the very beginning—on the third and following pages of the book—by giving us not one reason but two. First, time was heavy on his hands; he decided to write a book, any book—for example, a *History of the Suburbs* of Rio de Janeiro. In the following two sentences we are as much as told that this is not the real reason, for he gives us a second, more plausible, reason for writing his story: he will call to life certain ghosts or phantoms. He apostrophizes them with a quotation from *Faust:* "Ah there, are you come again, restless shades?" Why call up these shades? To bring back his youth, he says, and incidentally, this work will strengthen his hand for a more serious book.

But let us look at the last two sentences of the novel: "May the earth rest light on them! Let us turn to the *History of the Suburbs.*" These two sentences complete Santiago's stated reason for writing, which may now be paraphrased: "I will call up these restless shades and lay them once for all so that I can go peaceably about my business."

Why are the shades restless? Santiago does not explain. The ordinary belief is that the ghosts of murdered men return to haunt their murderers; and

Machado de Assis used this same quotation from *Faust* on another occasion in connection with murder victims.[1] Is Santiago a murderer? And who were these ghosts in life? As the narrative progresses they rise before the reader too. There is the young Bento, the good, generous, loving Bento, and all those who surrounded him—his mother, uncle, cousin, José Dias. There is Escobar—not only the young Escobar but the mature man as well. There is Capitú, growing ever more lovely to the day she died. And there is Ezekiel, the ingenuous, affectionate Ezekiel, true son of his mother and the Bento who might have been. Did Santiago murder them all? That would seem improbable. Two he did murder—by slow, tortured deaths—Bento and Capitú: the one spiritually, the other physically. And perhaps all the shades return to accuse him of these two murders.

Neither does Santiago explain why the act of narration will lay the ghosts. To lay bare the machinery of exorcism we must ask a further question—why did Santiago write his story *for publication?* Machado's other fictitious authors did not concern themselves with publication.[2] But Santiago refers to the publication of his story and printing details many times.[3] This is a question the reader must puzzle out for himself, though the answer is not hard to find.

Santiago received a degree from the justly famous law school at São Paulo. Even as a boy he kept Manduca entertained with his spirited defense of the Russians. His uncle was a criminal lawyer, and though his talents are belittled by Santiago, they were much admired by José Dias, and perhaps by others. Santiago was a practicing lawyer. But it is not until the final chapters of his story that his reason for publishing strikes us with full force. Chapters cxxxviii–cxl are permeated with the air of a courtroom. Capitú is in the dock. "She sat in a chair by the window. She may have been a trifle confused; her bearing was not that of an accused person." "Nature herself took the stand" against her. Santiago pours out legal phrases thick and fast: "admit," "deny," "courts," "witnesses for hire," "confession," "eye-witnesses," "pardon," "reparation," "justice," "paternity." In the final chapter (cxlviii), the reader realizes with a start that he has been pressed into jury duty. Santiago's "narrative" has been a long defense in his own behalf. With infinite pains he has established his own good character, his devoted love, kindness, truthfulness, and fairness. He has admitted to certain pardonable weaknesses such as jealousy, vanity, envy, susceptibility to female charms, and gullibility. And, clever lawyer that he is, he has undermined the character of every person in the case who could testify against him, suppressed evidence, got postponements till witnesses died. The argument runs as follows: he, Santiago, was not jealous without cause; he did not take an unjust revenge; Capitú was guilty. If his readers find him guiltless, he will be cleared in his own eyes, the restless shades will go back to their respective graves, and he can go with a clear conscience to his serious writings—the learned *History of the Suburbs,* and works on philosophy. Perhaps he will even find some pleasure with his despised mistresses.

He rests his case on Capitú's guilt. The last chapter is the final word to the jury: Capitú was deceitful to the core. One can almost hear him preface his closing words to his readers with the familiar *Gentlemen of the Jury,*

> If you remember Capitú the child, you will agree with me; you will have to acknowledge that the [later Capitú] was in the earlier, like the fruit within its rind.
>
> Well, whatever may be the solution, one fact remains and it is the sum of sums, the rest of the residuum, to wit, that my first love and my greatest friend, both so loving me, both so loved,

were destined to join together and deceive me . . .
May the earth rest light on them! Let us proceed
to the *History of the Suburbs*.

And the verdict?

As Santiago remarked prophetically at the beginning
of chapter xcviii, "Razão venceu," that is, "Reasoning
—legal argument—won." Nearly three generations, of
critics at least, have found Capitú guilty.

Let us reopen the case.

7

The Case for Capitú

THE SHAKESPEAREAN EDITOR William J. Rolfe wrote of
Desdemona: "The evidence furnished by 'honest Iago'
would have convicted her of infidelity in a court of
law."[1] The evidence furnished by "honest Santiago"
has convicted Capitú with many, if not most, readers;
but is it any more true than Iago's calumny?

The first witness against Capitú is José Dias. Through
his lips Santiago intimates that she was tricky and
ambitious, and out to get a rich, aristocratic husband—
Bento Santiago or some other. But José Dias later
repudiated his testimony, specifically in chapters c
and cxvi (and less explicitly elsewhere). He tells
Santiago: "I mistook childish ways for expression of
character and did not see that this mischievous little
girl with the pensive eyes was the capricious flower of
a sweet and wholesome fruit." Santiago counters by
showing that José Dias was a gullible fool, deceived
by her, by Bento, and by his own self-importance.
In making his closing statement, Santiago reverts to
José Dias's figure: she was always the same fruit, rotten
at the core; she deceived because she was deceitful by
nature. If this were so, surely she would have led a
life of excitement in Switzerland. Yet all indications
are against it. She lived there in seclusion (like Livia of
Resurreição), bringing up her son, loving Santiago,

writing him heart-broken letters, asking him to visit her Ezekiel, Santiago notes, believed in her.[2] We know that she was physically a strong, healthy woman, yet she died young (in her early forties), presumably of a broken heart, as the saying is, not from riotous living. It was Santiago who went in for that sort of thing. His soul, he tells us, did not remain in a corner like a pale, solitary flower, he lived the best he could—with mistresses to console him,[3] and good dinners, and theater parties.

There is another objection to accepting Santiago's statement without question: that objection is Machado de Assis, who, after all, *was* the creator of the characters in the book. As shown above, Machado de Assis believed the basis of a novel to be a struggle between contrasting natures, and in the criticism of *Primo Basílio,* from which I have already quoted, he particularly criticizes the heroine Luiza for commiting adultery with

> no moral reason, no passion, sublime or otherwise, no love, no resentment or anger, no perversion even, to explain it. Luiza slips into the mud without willing it, without struggle, without conscience . . . If Luiza is to attract and grip me, her tribulations must come from herself—let her be rebellious or repentant, let her suffer remorse or call down imprecations, but for God's sake let her have some moral fiber . . . There is no longer [any spiritual or emotional bond between her and us the readers] when she sickens and dies. Why? Because we know that the catastrophe is the result of a chance circumstance and nothing more; and for this reason, Luiza is not filled with remorse—she is frightened.

Santiago would have us believe that Capitú was another Luiza, that she committed adultery simply for the sake of deceiving, and that she feared the chance circumstance of Ezekiel's resemblance to Escobar

74

would disgrace her and separate her from her husband. But even if we accept Santiago's argument, Capitú does not lose her charm for us, just as she does not lose her charm for Santiago. Why? Because we do not really believe in her guilt, or not as he explains it— and neither does he.

The only tangible proof of Capitú's guilt that Santiago offers is the resemblance of the son Ezekiel to Escobar. This is the "handkerchief of Desdemona," this is the accessory that Santiago would make dominate the action. Who in the story notes this resemblance? Santiago and Capitú, also *possibly* Sancha, and *possibly* Escobar. No one else. José Dias, Santiago tells us, would have found Ezekiel the spit and image of him. Santiago says he fancied that Cousin Justina noticed it and he prevented her from seeing the grown Ezekiel because he did not want her to have the pleasure of confirming her suspicions. But could it not as easily have been the other way round, and he feared Justina would find that Ezekiel resembled him, or his mother, or father, or grandmother.

It was Santiago who first detected the resemblance, and announced it to Capitú in the following devious way:

"I find only one little defect in [Ezekiel]: he likes to imitate people."

"Imitate? In what way?"

"Imitate their gestures, their manners, their attitudes. He imitates Cousin Justina, he imitates José Dias; I've noticed that he has a way of moving his feet like Escobar, and his way of using his eyes . . ."

Capitú looked at me thoughtfully, and finally said we should correct him. For the first time, she realized it was a bad habit in the boy, but it seemed to her that it was only imitating for the sake of imitating, as many grown persons do who adopt the manners of others . . .

75

"And didn't you do it too when you were angry at some one?"

"When I was angry, I admit—a child's vengeance."[4]

In the light of Santiago's later charges and insinuations, *Capitú looked at me thoughtfully* seems like a confession of guilt; but consider what has gone before —chapter on chapter filled with Santiago's jealous moods, which even he acknowledges as unreasonable. Could it not be that Capitú, observing the sly way he led up to the point and broke off and perhaps something in his manner, thought: Now what? Is he going into one of his crazy fits of jealousy again?

And notice Santiago's admission: yes, he did imitate people as a child, and he was vengeful.

The next time the resemblance is hinted at is the chapter "Son of man," in which Santiago insinuated to José Dias that his mother had some reason for not visiting Capitú, and mentally reflected that she had been cold to her on recent visits to Dona Gloria— from which of course the reader is to infer that Dona Gloria had noticed something too.

In this little dramatic scene, as in the one described above, as in almost all those in the book, Santiago gives us the dialogue of all the actors with the attitudes and gestures of all but one, namely, his own. The reader, with the help of what Santiago discloses, or conceals, as to his feelings, must supply *his* gestures, attitude, tone of voice, and business.

A few moments after Santiago tried to sound out José Dias with his insinuation about Dona Gloria's coldness to Capitú (and incidentally got nowhere), José Dias turned his attention to the child Ezekiel and playfully called him his little prophet "son of man" "in the Biblical fashion." Santiago reports, minutely and dramatically, the irritation with which Capitú shut up José Dias, but any look, word, or gesture on his own part is omitted. The reader, however, recognizes this interplay as a direct insinuation that Ezekiel is a bastard: not the son of Santiago who is of divine lineage, but of Escobar who by name and description he has established as "son of man." Though Santiago omits his own reaction at the time, inner and outer, he has already primed the reader to sense his feelings: José Dias was right—Ezekiel was not a son of God, for he resembled not Bento who was the son of God by the Virgin Mary but Escobar who was man and son of man. It is reasonable to suppose that some of this feeling manifested itself in his face or in a gesture, and that Capitú noted it. By this time she was no doubt becoming more and more alarmed by the increasing frequency and blackness of Santiago's moods: she turned on José Dias and vented her despair and frustration in irritation against him for complicating her problem with his silly talk, for bringing on a mood in Santiago by his vain and garrulous display of learning and affection for Ezekiel. In the same manner, she reprimanded Ezekiel a few seconds later for his mischievousness, with perhaps uncalled-for severity. The effect of Capitú's resistance, ironically enough, only served to harden and confirm Santiago's "mood," and damn her in the eyes of the reader.

The coldness of Dona Gloria toward Capitú and Ezekiel was again thrown up, this time directly to Capitú, in chapter cxv, "Doubts on doubts." Because Capitú did not deny it does not mean that she acquiesced. Capitú almost never opposed or argued with Santiago. There were only two occasions when she put up any real resistance, and they were early in their love, when she called him a liar because he said he loved her more than his mother, and when she denied knowing the dandy. After their marriage she protested, but only slightly, against wearing long sleeves to balls. The rest of the time she gave in to Santiago's wishes, no matter how unreasonable. Even at the last when he made the charge that Escobar was the father of Ezekiel she did not deny it. But this attitude of Capitú's is well motivated. As Santiago recalls her, she appears to us a free, untrammeled mind, an aggressive, spirited girl—and she was—but she was also a woman brought up in the Portuguese tradition, which included strong oriental elements, from the Moors.[5] For example, Capitú's desire to learn Latin was laughed out of court by the gentle priest Cabral. Capitú herself bowed to the dictates of modesty in appearing at Santiago's house to congratulate the "Protonotary." After Santiago's first outburst of jealousy over the dandy, she herself offered to shut herself up in the harem as it were and not even look out the window. Later, she did that very thing, to calm Santiago's jealousy. Like a good Brazilian-Portuguese wife, she never "crossed" Santiago.

But the real motivation for all Capitú's acts was her love—her boundless love for Santiago and her pride in that love. It was her love which reinforced her wifeliness. She saved ten pounds sterling to show Bento what a good housewife she was. Though she was proud of her looks, loved jewels and clothes, she wanted to forego these: ". . . the only lace I'll ever wear is the husband of my heart." When Santiago lyingly told her his business was going badly, her response was immediate: sell her jewels, get rid of their expensive house. They could live in a shack till things got better. Everything would be all right.

Her love engendered patience—which was her undoing in the sight of the jealousy-hardened Santiago and in the eyes of his readers—her patience with his growing jealousy which she only vaguely understood and at first underestimated. She was all the more sympathetic with him because she too had known jealousy, jealousy of Dona Gloria as the first chapters show, and of Sancha too, as witness her remark when Santiago told her he and Escobar had agreed that their wives should wear long sleeves to balls: "Sanchinha's arms are not shapely." Does this remark not indicate that she was hurt that Bento should not trust her love, and a hurt pride tinged with jealousy that he should compare her in any respect with Sancha? That the remark was not absolutely true and that Capitú's jealousy had some foundation we learn thirteen chapters later ("The hand of Sancha"), when Santiago admits to a sexual interest in Sancha dating from a long time before, and further admits that when Escobar asked him to feel his muscle, "I felt his arms as if I were feeling Sancha's." But Capitú's resentment, as always, was short-lived and, as usual, she acceded to Santiago's unreasonable demand with her usual gentle patience. And how did Santiago reward this gentle patience which he describes in chapter after chapter? He labels it "the fine art of Capitú."[6] In the same way, Othello, when worked upon by Iago, called Desdemona "that cunning whore of Venice."

As with Desdemona, her love, because of its self-abandonment, gave rise to despair. As long as she did not know the cause of Santiago's moods, she tried to combat them with love, to win him to his old love. When she was faced with the final brutal charge of adultery, she was helpless: what good would a denial do? With melancholy dignity—pride and despair—she bowed to destiny: "It is the will of God."

It was her pride, her *augusta-capitolina* quality which made her reject the only possible way of saving her marriage—an appeal to her mother-in-law. Santiago does not make this clear in so many words, but at this point he makes one of his unexplained statements: after repeating that it was the will of God, she went off to church, and he awaited her return. "It was more delayed than usual [he writes]; I began to fear that she had gone to my mother's, but she had not." Why did he fear that Capitú had gone to his mother's? He gives no explanation. But the reader must. This is one of the "lacunae" Santiago mentions in an early chapter where he cautions his readers against gaps in his book, caused by his "poor memory."

79

And rather forgetfulness than confusion! . . . There is no way of emending a confused book, but everything may be supplied in the case of books with omissions. For my part, when I read one of the latter type I am not bothered a bit. What I do, on arriving at the end, is to shut my eyes and evoke all the things which I did not find in it. How many fine ideas come to me then! What profound reflections! The rivers, mountains, churches, which I did not find on the written page, all now appear to me with their waters, their trees, their altars; and the generals draw swords that never left their scabbards, and the clarion releases notes that slept in the metal, and everything marches with sudden soul.

The fact is, everything is to be found outside a book that has gaps, gentle reader. This is the way I fill in other men's lacunae; in the same way you may fill in mine.[7]

How are we to fill in Santiago's lacuna? If Capitú had gone to her mother-in-law with Santiago's charge, Dona Gloria would have pronounced it ridiculous (perhaps also the resemblance of Ezekiel to Escobar) and asserting her old authority would have made her "dutiful" son return to the path of reason. Is this why Santiago was afraid Capitú had gone to his mother's house? And with the carte blanche Santiago has given us we can close our eyes and fill in further details: Dona Gloria was convinced, like José Dias, that Ezekiel resembled Bento, Santiago had already started to run around with other women and Cousin Justina had got wind of it; and so on, ad infinitum. And Capitú? Why did she reject an appeal to Dona Gloria? Because she was proud, because her only weapon was her love—she met every rebuff with love—and because of despair, for her love no longer had any power against Santiago's hard heart: if Bento would not trust her and love her for herself she would not force him through his mother—and anyway it would be of no use. She would go on loving the Bento that was dead and weep for the unfortunate man who killed him.[8] There was probably also a small element of false pride in Capitú's rejection of Dona Gloria's help, because of a residue of the old feeling of jealousy against her, but there was probably also a tinge of pity, a mother's pity for this mother who was a failure. And there was Capitú's love for her own son Ezekiel.

In the words of Santiago, we must "reconstruct" the white heat of Santiago's jealousy, we must "reconstruct" the towering tide of Capitú's love. And then the clarion of truth will release notes that sleep in the metal and everything will march with sudden soul. That is to say, Capitú was not a "puppet" like Eça's Luiza: she was animated by her love, with its pride, jealousy, and despair—however much Santiago belittles that love—and from it resulted her actions, whatever those actions were.

But this is only one way of filling in Santiago's lacuna. Let us return to his cold legal charge that Ezekiel resembled Escobar. As we have seen, Santiago discovered it. Capitú came to believe in it, even to regard it with superstitious awe: the chance resemblance was "the will of God." Perhaps she meant by this that she, as well as Santiago, was being punished for her part in the breaking of Dona Gloria's oath. In the same way, in *Othello* it was Othello who "lost" the handkerchief, made Desdemona drop it on the floor to be found by Emilia and used by Iago—and Desdemona believed Othello's lie about its mystic origin and properties, and that it was she who had lost it, though it was Othello and her loving concern for Othello which lost it.

There are two other persons who seemed to note the resemblance. In the chapter "Friends and neighbors" (cxvii) Santiago tells us that the two youngsters Ezekiel and Capitùzinha passed their days together

81

and that he happened to remark in the presence of Capitú, Sancha, and Escobar, that *they* might fall in love as had he and his childhood companion Capitú. . . . Sancha added that they were even getting to look alike. I explained:

"No, it's because Ezekiel imitates the gestures of other people."

Escobar agreed with me, and suggested that sometimes children who are always together finally come to look alike.

From this we, the readers, are to infer: Ezekiel looks like Capitùzinha; children resemble their fathers, hence Capitùzinha looks like Escobar; Ezekiel looks like Escobar; Escobar and Sancha admit it. But do they? All that Sancha and Escobar say is that Ezekiel looks like Capitùzinha—who for all we know may look like Santiago, for there is no description of her appearance. (Or, since Sancha's mother resembled Capitú, why should not the granddaughter resemble Capitú's son?)

As for Sancha, who is the one to notice the resemblance between the children, may she not have been motivated by a jealousy similar to Santiago's? As a girl she had been attracted to him, as he to her. Recall the scene "After Mass" (chap. lxx), how she made a great commotion about waylaying him to ask after his mother; and how Santiago noticed she was "not bad looking," had a cute nose, and her style of dress, and remarked that it was a day of pleasant *surprises* (plural) though the only other surprise that day was a visit from Escobar. Forty-eight chapters later ("The hand of Sancha") we find Sancha and Santiago (according to his account) actually ogling each other and squeezing each other's hands. And he admits he had one day "thought of her as one thinks of the fair unknown who passes by," and that he suspected she had known and even returned his sentiments. Even without this attraction to Santiago, Sancha had reason to envy the beautiful and capable Capitú whom Escobar as well as Santiago admired. And if there was gossip of an affair between Escobar and an actress, as Santiago reports, she had reason to suspect her husband.

Escobar's remark about the children, I believe, has not so much a psychological cause as a logical one. That Escobar loved Capitú is not inconceivable: the symbolism surrounding his drowning may even bear out Machado de Assis's intention on this point. And how could he help loving her? The other characters in the book all fell under her spell. We all love Capitú. Sancha was scarcely more significant or, from Santiago's hints, more admirable than Cassio's Bianca. But that Escobar expressed his love to Capitú or that Capitú loved him, this I no more believe than that Desdemona loved Cassio—except that Capitú's love, like Juliet's, "as boundless as the sea," encompassed all those who loved Bento and were loved by him. She probably had a particular feeling of sympathy and gratitude for Escobar (as Desdemona was grateful to Cassio), for he had been the go-between for her and Bento and had encouraged their love. And Escobar displayed the protective attitude of a big brother toward Capitú, whom he called his "little sister-in-law." Early in the story when she was faced with the problem of combating Dona Gloria's influence over Bento, Capitú mentally ran over the persons who might help her and lighted upon José Dias because he was the most capable, and devoted to Bento. Now, when she was faced with the problem of combating the influence of Casmurro over Bento—that is, his strange moods and suspicions—it would be natural, perhaps even inevitable, that she should turn to Escobar, who was also capable and devoted to Bento.

Desdemona, in her trouble and confusion, turned to Iago: "O good Iago,/What shall I do to win my lord again?/Good friend, go to him; for, by this light of heaven,/I know not how I lost him"; but if Cassio had been a strong man instead of a weak one, would she not have turned to him? Capitú, as the accusation scene proves, did not herself fully understand the basis of Santiago's jealous moods: how could she have explained them to, say, José Dias or Dona Gloria, or even convinced them of the existence of any serious trouble? But Escobar was a man of the world; he knew and understood Bento as probably no one else did; his powers of observation and ratiocination, his level-headedness—"2 + 2 = 4"—are established beyond any question, as also his gift for getting others to see things his way. Besides, he was an affectionate "big brother" to Capitú and Bento. For my part, I believe Capitú confided her problem to Escobar, that he recognized the seriousness of it and tried to help her. This would explain Capitú's going secretly to Escobar about the ten pounds sterling, and Escobar's appearing at Santiago's house when he was at the theater, and Escobar's thoughtfulness during his conversation with Santiago on both those occasions. It is to be noted too that these two incidents were immediately preceded (in the narration) by fits of jealousy on Santiago's part—jealousy of nothing, as he admits. It would explain Santiago's later recollections of finding Capitú and Escobar alone in conversation and their constraint on these occasions. It would explain Capitú's sadness when she looked at the dead Escobar—if indeed it needs to be explained—and her bursting into tears when his posthumous letter to Bento was read: she had lost not only a friend but her *tábua de salvação*—her only hope of salvation in shipwreck. Escobar had "strong arms," "powerful lungs," he could swim in the sea of love.

To repeat, Escobar's abilities in the way of observation and deduction were extraordinary, and if his attention had been directed to Santiago's "moods" by Capitú, Santiago's casual insinuations would not be lost on him, nor Santiago's interest in Sancha, or

Sancha's in Santiago for that matter. Thus, when Sancha remarked that the children looked alike and Santiago added that it was because Ezekiel imitated other people, Escobar would recognize what both were driving at—even though they themselves were not consciously aware of their intention. Hence his conciliatory and rather banal remark that children who are always together come to resemble each other: it was to clear the air, bring the conversation to a sane, common sense basis—in short, to help Capitú.

In the final analysis, Santiago is the main witness for the "resemblance"—and, as José Veríssimo wrote, his testimony is "suspect" because of his love and hate.[9] Sancha apparently saw it, but she too is "suspect." Capitú saw it, but this may have been the power of Santiago's suggestion working on her. There is no evidence that anyone else noted the resemblance, not even the hawk-eyed Justina; there is definite indication that Dona Gloria[10] and José Dias did *not* see it.[11]

But grant the resemblance. In what did it consist? Santiago would have us believe that Ezekiel resembled Escobar from top to toe, inside and out, in manners and in mind. His voice was the same, his table manners, his talkativeness, his flair for mathematics, his memory, his business ability, his sadistic tendencies (both he and Escobar liked to kill mice). The only difference Santiago concedes is that Ezekiel, the grown Ezekiel, was shorter than Escobar and not of as sturdy build. (It might be recalled that Santiago was shorter even than Capitú, and not muscular or athletic.) Leaving aside the thoughts and observations that Santiago confides to the reader, what is the viva-voce testimony of Machado de Assis's characters on this point? We have the words of Bento to Capitú: Ezekiel has the same manner of moving his feet and using his eyes as Escobar because he imitates Escobar (and Santiago shows conclusively that Ezekiel was a mimic). We

85

have the words of Capitú, who called Bento's attention to the odd expression of Ezekiel's eyes—an expression like Escobar's and that of a friend of Padua's. And that is all! In other words, the resemblance resolves into a manner of moving the feet and of using the eyes—both of which habits might easily have been acquired through imitation as Santiago first suggested. We who are party to Santiago's inmost feelings know that this "imitation" is quite as unpalatable to him as a real, physical resemblance—for imitation is a sincere form of flattery and would mean that Ezekiel wanted to be like Escobar. (Nowhere does Santiago state that Ezekiel imitated *him*.) It will be recalled that Santiago never mentions Ezekiel's affection for Capitú, for example, without adding "but he was more fond of me."[12] Even when Ezekiel returned to Rio de Janeiro, the hardened Casmurro was touched by the young man's effusive love and trust. And Santiago, in frequent moments of confidence, confesses his "vanity."

But, for the sake of argument, let us grant a genuine resemblance. It is our clever lawyer Santiago, himself, who brings up the only objection we could make—coincidence—and demolishes it; not with logic and evidence, but with sarcasm and *casmurricity*. Gurgel, the father of Sancha, had called the young Santiago's attention to Capitú's resemblance to his dead wife's portrait. People who had known his wife

> said the same thing. He too thought the features similar, especially the forehead and the eyes. As for their natures they were one . . .
> . . . "Sometimes, in life [said Gurgel], there are these strange resemblances."[13]

Some dozen pages from the end of the book Santiago reminds us of this oracular dictum of Gurgel's:

> Meantime I had recalled the words of the late Gurgel that time at his house when he showed me the portrait of his wife, which resembled Capitú.

86

You must remember them; if not, reread the chapter. I do not place the number of it here, because I no longer remember which it is, but it cannot be far back. They boil down to this: there are these inexplicable resemblances . . .[14]

And he goes on with his suspicions and insinuations. Though admitting Capitú's resemblance to the portrait, he contemptuously rejects Gurgel's dictum that there are accidental resemblances, and sarcastically tells us, the jury, to go back and read over Gurgel's testimony if we want to consider such superstitious rubbish. This is the import of his words. And we, the jury, are deterred by his sarcasm, for he has already discredited Gurgel in our eyes by painting him as a garrulous, low class, vulgar man with a coarse nose and a pot belly who was foolishly fond of his daughter, that is, as a person for whose opinion no one of sense and refinement will have any regard. On the other hand, Santiago has conditioned us to accept a contrary superstition, namely, that sons always resemble their fathers. This belief was insinuated into the reader's mind by the chapter "The son is the image of his father," in which Dona Gloria got her brother to admit that her son resembled his dead father (just as Gurgel had got Santiago to agree that Capitú resembled the portrait of his wife), for *boa vida* Cosme never disagreed with anything Gloria said: "Yes, there is something, the eyes, the shape of the face."

Did Santiago resemble his father? We have only Dona Gloria's word for it. Santiago had told us his father was tall, with hair curled in close ringlets, his air confident, his manner forthright and somewhat cavalier.[15] Santiago, on the contrary, seems to have been short,[16] with comparatively straight hair,[17] a repressed manner,[18] and his narrative is a history of his "doubts." The reader might perhaps later recall these discrepancies, were it not that this chapter foreshadows another, in which Capitú points out the resemblance between Ezekiel and the dead Escobar. Even the words of the later scene echo those of the earlier one:

> "Brother Cosme, he's the image of his father isn't he?"
>
> "Yes, there is something, the eyes . . ."
>
> ". . . But take a good look, Brother Cosme, see if he isn't the picture of my dear departed. Look this way, Bentinho, look at me . . ."[19]

and:

> "Have you noticed that Ezekiel has an odd expression about the eyes?" asked Capitú. "I've seen only two other people with the same expression, a friend of Papa's and the dear departed Escobar. Look Ezekiel, look straight, there, look at Papa . . ."[20]

As Santiago intended, the inference is not lost on his jury.

It might be profitable, though, to consider what Machado de Assis's opinion may have been in this matter. In the novel *Esaú e Jacob*, we find a young heroine who not only bears no resemblance to either her mother or her father but is in complete conflict with them, body and soul. In presenting her to the reader, the narrator of that novel—who, by the way, bears much more resemblance to his creator than ever Santiago did—makes this explanation:

> Children do not always reproduce their parents. Camões claimed that from a certain father one could only expect a son of the same sort, and science confirms this poetic rule. For my part I believe in science as in poetry, but there are exceptions, my friend. It happens at times that nature does something quite different, and not for this reason do the plants stop growing and the stars shining. What one must believe without fail is that God is God . . .[21]

Even in *Dom Casmurro*, Gurgel uttered the dictum, "Sometimes, in life, there are these strange resem-

88

blances." And Gurgel was as much Machado de Assis's creation as is Santiago. We have more reason to trust his opinion, for he had no ulterior motive in making his casual observation, and was not blinded by passion, as Santiago is.

No, we of the jury, have fallen under the spell of a persuasive attorney. We have done worse: we have given free rein to our own suspicious natures—for we all have within us a strain of "casmurro." In the novel *Quincas Borba*, Machado de Assis (who is its narrator), after recounting a train of circumstantial evidence pointing to an *affair* between the heroine and *another*, which whips the jealousy of the protagonist Rubião into a frenzy, rebukes the reader in the following words:

> [The trouble is] the reader lost his way and could not fit together Sophia's hurt anger with the cabdriver's tale; and so asks in bewilderment, "Then the rendez-vous of Rua da Harmonia, Sophia, Carlos Maria—this tinkling flim-flam of sweet, guilty-sounding rhymes—is all calumny?"
>
> All calumny—the reader's and Rubião's, not the poor cabby's, for he mentioned no names, was not even reporting an actual case. You would have seen this for yourself if you had read slowly and reflectively. Yes, benighted reader, only consider: it would be highly improbable for a man going on an *adventure* of the sort to have the cab wait in front of the hideaway. It would establish a witness to the crime. There are more streets in heaven and earth than are dreamt of in your philosophy—cross-streets where the cab could have waited very nicely.[22]

We too, benighted readers of *Dom Casmurro*, have permitted our own suspicious natures to add to and confirm the suspicions of Santiago. The fact—if it be a fact—that Ezekiel bore a resemblance to Escobar does not necessarily lead to the conclusion that Ezekiel was Escobar's son.

89

Gurgel is not the only oracle flouted by Santiago. There is another more solemn one declaring the true origin of Ezekiel, nothing less than the Good Book itself: "Thou wast perfect in thy ways from the day that thou was created"—on which Santiago casts skeptical disbelief with his question, "When would have been the day of Ezekiel's creation?" But we had best heed the rebuke administered by Machado de Assis, and take this Biblical quotation solemnly. If we do, it means Ezekiel was the true born son of Santiago, Capitú innocent, Santiago a jealous infidel.[23] It means Escobar was "perfect in his ways," for he too was named Ezekiel, and it was Machado de Assis who gave him that name.

So much for the accessory which Santiago manipulates to such purpose. If one takes away the testimony of the resemblance what is left to the case against Capitú? If you take away the handkerchief of Desdemona, wrote Machado de Assis, there remains Iago's calumny, the jealous soul of Othello, the innocence of Desdemona—these are the ingredients of the tragedy.

Though Santiago makes the claim that Capitú was born to deceive, the fact remains: *if* she deceived her husband with Escobar, it was Casmurro she deceived, not Bento. Santiago calls our attention to this fact in his last chapter: "If Jesus son of Sirach had known of my first fits of jealousy, he would have said to me, as in his Ch. IX, vs. 1: 'Be not jealous of thy wife lest she set herself to deceive thee with the malice that she learnt of thee.'" Then he dismisses the possibility from our minds as preëmptorily as he dismissed the two oracles: "But I do not believe it was so, and you will agree with me." Oh, we will? Santiago's jealousy appeared early, in all its force and ugliness, and steadily ate away the Bento in him: it appeared before Capitú knew of Escobar's existence, or he of hers. Earlier still. When the "casmurro" in

Santiago hearkened to José Dias's insinuation that Capitú's eyes were sly and tricky, he went and looked into those eyes, found "nothing extraordinary in them, their color and gentleness were [his] old friends." In these first scenes Santiago lets us see Capitú as she appeared to Bento: the age of Juliet, beautiful, intelligent, spirited, passionate and affectionate, her love —like Juliet's—as deep and infinite as the sea. And Bento returned her love, though *his* love was not so great as hers. His dreams were not so beautiful as hers.[24] He could eat sweets in the midst of the threat of eternal separation, for he was the true nephew of Uncle Cosme, whom one cannot imagine missing a meal for anything. Yet, momentarily, he was swept on out of himself by the tide in her eyes: but he struggled—pulled back by his ego and by the bond that held him to his mother.

No, says Casmurro, Capitú's soul was not love, but deceit. Deceit welled up naturally in her, and he echoes Iago: she deceived her father, and her mother as well, and my mother and all our household. It is true, when Capitú was faced with Dona Gloria's threat of keeping Bento for herself by making a priest of him, she gave way to angry frustration and jealousy. She conceived a plan to get him away from his mother, send him over the sea to Europe, "and leave my mother standing on the sand." Again the figure of the sea, representing her love.

She persuaded Bento to join her in a patient, painstaking plot to circumvent Dona Gloria. She had to *persuade* Santiago for two reasons. Being, as we have said, the true nephew of Cosme, anything in the painstaking line was not his style. Wishing was Santiago's way out of all difficulties, praying to the indulgent God who had miraculously arranged his birth and naturally would take care of everything else for him. Secondly, his love for Capitú was not sufficient to make him go to work of his own will (it was only the next day he told his mother with hasty grammar, "I only love you, Mamma"): he was a divided soul, a large part of him still wanted to be a priest and remain true to the "Santíssima" Dona Gloria.

It was not only the young Capitú's "plot" which Santiago traced to an inborn gift for deceit, there was also the ease with which she covered up the first and second kiss.

> Capitú was mistress of herself not only in the presence of her mother; her father did not frighten her one whit more. In the midst of a situation which left me tongue-tied, she talked away with the greatest ingenuousness in this world. My belief is that her heart beat neither faster nor slower. She claimed to be startled and put on a half-scared look; but I, who knew the whole story, saw that it was false, and I envied her.[25]

Santiago envied her, but he shows conclusively that it was not her ability *to deceive* that he envied, but something quite different. Santiago, even the young Santiago, had well-defined gifts in that line. The key to Santiago's envy is to be found in the attitude in which the reader first sees him—hiding behind the door. This first view of him looks forward to a much later chapter, "A comparison," in which we find him in the same attitude; but here the attitude is explained. In the later chapter, Santiago compares his sufferings to those of Priam, and concludes that there were no Homers in his day because

> the Priams hide themselves in obscurity and silence. Their tears, if they shed them, are wiped away behind the door so that their faces may appear bright and clean. Their talk is rather of joy than of melancholy, and all goes along as if Achilles had not killed Hector.

In other words, the young Santiago repressed his feelings—especially his hatred—as the older Santiago repressed his feelings of jealousy and hatred. The young Santiago loved his "saintly" and beautiful mother but he also hated her for sacrificing him to God, and he was no doubt jealous of her devotion to God, of her attentions to her dead husband, to José Dias, Justina, and the others. But only once did this hatred manifest itself in an undisguised emotion: the wish for her death. Elsewhere it was disguised. When Capitú learned of Dona Gloria's decision to send Bento to the seminary, her anger burst forth naturally and directly against Dona Gloria. Bento's vengeful anger, on the contrary, was directed against José Dias, who was not the cause, only the occasion, of the threatened separation. Six chapters later ("Mother and servant"), we learn that Santiago identified José Dias with his mother: in venting his anger against José Dias he was using him as a whipping boy for her.

When Santiago first kissed Capitú he was assailed with feelings of guilt—guilt at betraying his mother and God—which made him as fearfully anxious in the presence of her mother and father as if they had been *his* mother and Father. Even after he was grown, he did not want José Dias as go-between for his letters to Capitú "because of a residue of childish feelings of awe."

Swept forward by the surge of Capitú's love, Santiago banished his feelings of guilt by identifying Capitú with God and with his mother. Capitú was an "altar"[26] and "the angel of the Scriptures."[27] He dreamed of living with her in a house like his mother's,[28] he discovered in her the same traits of character as in his mother,[29] and when he married he went to live in Gloria. In this transference he was assisted by both his mother[30] and Capitú,[31] who identified themselves with each other: Capitú became "the flower" of Dona Gloria's house, and his name "was between the two women like the watchword of the life to come."

But no matter where Santiago transferred his love,

there he also transferred his hate. Like Cousin Justina, he suspected the disinterestedness of everyone's love for him—not only his mother's, but José Dias's, Escobar's, Padua's, and all the others', and principally, of course, Capitú's. "I was a well of doubts," he tells us.[32] These doubts, however, were not of anything outside himself, for they began to appear at the outset, when he noticed that Capitú was more beautiful than he, that her dreams were more beautiful than his, her loving concern greater than his, the power of her love greater than any fear. His doubts were actually one—doubt of his ability to love. This doubt engendered in him other doubts of a more specific nature: as, doubt of his own manhood—Capitú conceived but once, *he* could not have begotten Ezekiel;[33] as, doubt that Capitú would prefer him to Escobar, who was taller, more muscular, more handsome, more brainy, more charming, and so on. But the big doubt remained—doubt of his own love. He confesses his defections—his interest in Escobar's sister, in other girls, in Sancha, and finally his mistresses. It is noteworthy that his first outburst of vengeful jealousy against Capitú was preceded by a vague interest in Escobar's sister, his second, greater outburst, by his eying Sancha after Mass, and the greatest outburst, at the funeral of Escobar, by his advances to Sancha the night before. That is to say, he projected his own defections upon Capitú, and, throughout, his doubt of self represented itself to him as doubt of Capitú.

When Santiago says he envied Capitú her heaven-sent ability to deceive,[34] he means he envied Capitú her faith, her confidence, the singleness, the purity, the self-abandonment of her love. For Capitú felt no guilt, no shame, in loving Bento. She loved her father and mother, but as Santiago puts it, ". . . she loved me more or in another way";[35] and this love for Bento prompted her to the bold stratagem he calls "deceit" —as Desdemona's love for Othello emboldened her to "deceive her father," and "seel [his] eyes up close as oak," so that he thought it "witchcraft." Like Desdemona, Capitú battled the jealousy of Bento and the machinations of Casmurro with love and love's faith. That was her crime.

When Santiago, in his final chapter, clinches his argument to the reader with the statement that the early Capitú was in the later, ironically, he speaks true. Capitú does not change, as Desdemona does not change. Othello changes. "The Moor already changes with my poison," says Iago. Bento changes with Casmurro's poison: "there was a new man within me, the creation of new and strong pressures."[36] Nothing changed Capitú—neither coldness, rebuffs, cruelty, nor abuse. She died loving her Othello. Though Santiago murdered her, she is not really dead—either for him or for us the readers. Like Manduca, she represents love's victory over death. It is not for nothing that Machado's creature Santiago envelops her in symbols of the sea, for his creator was familiar with the Greek myth that Venus was born of the sea, and he was familiar with the Camoensian addition, that Venus was mother of the Portuguese race. Capitú is pure Portuguese womanhood, love incarnate struggling against self-love (Casmurro) for the soul (Bento) of Santiago—for the essential part of the soul is love.

8

Some Symbols

IN MANDUCA we found love, life, and the spirit of
Jesus equated. We saw too that Santiago did not interpret Manduca for us in quite the same way, but, on
the contrary, as the "devil" and as "hog manure"
that nourished the flower Bento. Neither does Santiago
interpret Capitú as "love" but as something more
nearly representing lust, evil, earth, the devil. But
wary old legal fox that he is, he is also a criminal before the bar, with a criminal's perverse desire to confess, even brag of his crime. We will find by a close
examination of the symbolism running through his
narrative that, not only does his interpretation fall
down, but some of his other metaphors and explanations confirm the interpretation I suggested in the
foregoing chapter.

The symbolism in *Dom Casmurro* appears, and is,
elaborate. But, as Freud demonstrated for dreams,
though the elaboration may be so manifold as to defy
cataloguing, the wish which gives rise to the protean
forms of the dream may be quite simple—so, in
Dom Casmurro the manifold symbolism on close inspection proves to be only many ways of saying pretty
much the same thing.

The House

The first major symbol is contained in the title *Dom
Casmurro*. Since, however, we have already given

"casmurro" some consideration, let us pass on for the present to the second—the house as a symbol for the soul ("a person's soul . . . is arranged like a house")[1] —which first occurs in chapter ii. Santiago tells us he tried to reconstruct the old house where he passed his childhood and adolescence and thus bring back his youth. And who destroyed the old house? In chapter cxliv he says, "You will ask why, when I had the old house itself, in the same ancient street, I let them tear it down and came and reproduced it here." His answer is this: after his mother died, he went to the old house, but "the whole house disowned" him; that is, Bento disowned Dom Casmurro—Dr. Jekyll repudiated Mr. Hyde. "It was all strange and hostile," he says, "I let them tear it down." Now here is a magnificent "lacuna": let *whom* tear it down? It was his property. We can only conclude that he means the wreckers whom he, Santiago, hired to tear it down. In other words, Hyde put the finishing touches to Jekyll; Casmurro completed the murder of Bento.[2] Then he tried to restore the old house in a new location. Location in space is symbolical for location in time: ". . . my purpose was to tie together the two ends of my life, to restore adolescence in old age." That is, he tried to resurrect his soul, his "Bento." He tells us he did not succeed: he succeeded only in raising a tomb with a well-embalmed corpse ("I myself am missing. What is here . . . may be likened to dye on hair and beard: it barely preserves the outer *habit* as they say in autopsies"), a monument housing a "retrospective exhibition" and haunted by ghosts. This is the same symbolism employed by Machado de Assis in his first novel *Resurreição* ("his heart, if it rose from the dead for a few days, has forgotten in the tomb its feeling of trust and moments of fleeting ecstasy").

Though at times the "house" symbol seems to be used by Santiago with a slightly different meaning, it is really the same with the emphasis on the essential part of the soul—love—as when Santiago explains that his soul was like a house with no locks and keys and that Escobar pushed open the door and entered—that is, entered his friendship, confidence, and love. In the same way, Santiago's story was: he lived in his mother's house, married and lived in Capitú's house, in Escobar's, and Escobar in his; then he frequented boarding houses (mistresses and gay companions),[3] and finally tried to return to his mother's.

Before we leave this symbol, perhaps we should take a look at some of the house's furnishings. Santiago particularly mentions the washing-stones and gardens, recalling slavery; the portraits of his mother and father; the decoration of the living-room walls—flowers supported in space by sturdy birds, with the four seasons in the corners (his narrative begins with the late-spring of his life, also of the year, and ends with winter); and the four Roman medallions, Caesar, Augustus, Nero, and Masinissa, which inspired him to write his narrative. ("The busts painted on the wall spoke to me and said that since they had failed to bring back the days gone by, I should take my pen and tell over those times.")

"The reason for these personages," says Santiago, "eludes me"—another magnificent "lacuna" on our fictitious author's part—and yet he refers to them four different times.[4] What elements in his soul do they represent? The first three were Romans, the fourth an African ally of the Romans who gave up his wife to remain with them. They were all men of wealth and power. The only one elaborated upon by Santiago is Caesar, whose greatness, it would seem, resided in his love of a woman.[5] Perhaps this is the key to part of the meaning of the other three: the uxorious Augustus loved Livia Augusta to distraction; Nero loved his mother with an incestuous love and murdered her to marry the adulterous Poppaea; Masinissa sent his wife Sophonisba a dish of poison which she quaffed without hesitation, but also not without sarcasm.[6] Consider Capitú's final words to Santiago.

> Capitú could not help laughing . . . Then in a tone half ironic, half melancholy, "And even dead men! Not even the dead escape your jealousy! . . . I confided all my bitterness to God," said Capitú on her return from church. "I heard within me the answer that our separation is inevitable, and I am at your disposal."

And it may be—must be—significant that after Ezekiel's return from Europe and the death of Capitú, Santiago finds him staring at the bust of Masinissa.[7]

The Flower, Worms, and Sonnet

The third major symbol "the flower" is introduced as part of the decoration of the house, the garlands painted on the wall, and, more specifically, in the description of the two portraits.

> The portrait of my mother shows she was beautiful. She was twenty then and held a flower between her fingers. In the picture she seems to offer the flower to her husband . . . They are portraits that could pass for originals. The one of my mother, holding the flower toward her husband, seems to say: "I am all yours, my gallant cavalier!" That of my father, looking out at us, makes this commentary, "See how the girl loves me."

The meaning of the symbol seems quite clear: love—youthful, pure, self-abandoned love.[8]

The subject of the sonnet Santiago never finished was "flower of heaven bright and pure." "What was the flower?" Santiago asks, and answers, "Capitú, probably." Then he passes on to other concepts: "virtue," "poetry," "religion," "freedom," "justice," and ends with "charity" ("caridade"). "Caridade" is defined by Caldas Aulete[9] as "love of one's fellow-man; one of the three theologic virtues by which we love

99

God as our supreme good and our fellow-man as ourselves; a good heart, goodness." Again, "flower" symbolizes "love," and "flower of heaven," "Christian love of one's fellow-man and of God." From his indecision over the last line of the sonnet, we perceive that Bento identified himself and his soul with the "flower." Shall it be "Life is lost, the battle still is won!" or "Life is won, the battle still is lost!"—with "life" signifying "life in this world," "life of the flesh"? Should he, Bento, the son of the "Santíssima" Gloria and God, win the battle of heaven by remaining true to his mother and God as a priest, or lose it by marrying Capitú, the flesh and the devil? This seems to have been Santiago's interpretation. We have already received preliminary hints of Santiago's identifying himself with the "flower of heaven bright and pure." Capitú called him a flower (chapter xii);[10] and in chapter li he told us, "I was pure, pure I remained and pure I entered the halls of São José." Later, in the Manduca episode, nature beckoned to the "loathsome" Manduca with the "flower" Bento and thus the flower took on beauty. And Manduca was "hog manure" that nourished "the violet" Bento and increased his "fragrance." (Santiago recognized the good influence of Manduca on his soul.)

Capitú was also "the flower," as Santiago first suggests in his chapter on the sonnet (lv). In chapter lxxx, the figure is repeated: "Capitú came to be the flower of [my mother's] house, the sun of its mornings, the cool of its evenings, the moon of its nights"—in other words the essential part of the soul (the house) is love (the flower).[11] And José Dias referred to the child Capitú as "the capricious flower of a sweet and wholesome fruit."

Both Capitú and the "Bento" in Santiago are "the flower," for they are the same. In the next to the last chapter of his book, Santiago tells us: "You already

100

PENNSYLVANIA MILITARY COLLEGE
CHESTER, PENNSYLVANIA
LIBRARY

know that my soul, however lacerated, did not remain in a corner like a pale, solitary flower . . . I lived the best I could and not without the company of women." We also know that Capitú's soul did remain in a corner like a pale, solitary flower. The flower that was Capitú continued to bloom in the barren cold of Switzerland. The "Bento" in Santiago was dead: the same thing happened to Santiago's "flower" as happened to his "house"—Casmurro destroyed it.

In other writings of Machado de Assis's the "flower" (heart, love, soul, life) is destroyed by a "worm" which is identified as "jealousy," "cynicism," "death."[12] The "worm" in *Dom Casmurro* is not brought into immediate contact with the "flower," but, I believe, the reader is justified in making the connection. Chapter xvii, "The worms," would seem extraneous to the narrative were it not for the two symbols, "the lance of Achilles" (God, life)[13] and "the worms" (death). The worms in this instance are gnawing books. But a book in Machado's language is a man's "life of the spirit,"[14] which comes close in meaning to "the flower." And this chapter "The worms" prepares us for the two later chapters (lxii and lxxiii) in which jealousy sinks its tooth into Bento. (That the worm has become a serpent makes it no less a worm, as Santiago would say.) Thus by a triple series of hints and lacunae, Casmurro is identified with the "worm" (jealousy, death), which attacked "the flower Bento" (love, soul).

The line which Bento chose as the final verse to his sonnet predicts the outcome of the book: "Life is won, the battle still is lost!" "For whosoever will save his life shall lose it; but whosoever shall lose his life for my sake and the gospel's, the same shall save it. For what shall it profit a man, if he shall gain the whole world, and lose his own soul?"[15] Bento Santiago lost his soul. Hence the symbolism of the sonnet is the same as that of the house: he could not connect the first verse and the last because the essence of his soul was gone.

The Dream and the Dramatic Reform

Again, the message of the broken dream which Bento could not put together or restore is the same as that of the "house" and the "sonnet," as Santiago specifically states.

> You know that this house in Engenho Novo, in its dimensions, arrangement and decoration is the reproduction of my old Matacavallos house. And as I told you in Chapter 2, my purpose in recreating the other house was to link together the two ends of my life, which, by the way, I have not accomplished. Well, the same thing happened to that dream at the seminary.[16]

Even the dream element, the lottery ticket bearing the number 4004, contains the same symbolism as the house, the sonnet, and the broken dream: an identical integer at the beginning and the end, separated by a blank.

In the second chapter on the dream ("An idea and a scruple"), Santiago carefully explains that dreams originate in a person's brain; even before this (chapter xxx) he explained that dreams weave themselves on the pattern of our inclinations and recollections. In other words, Bento's dream was a divided wish: he wanted both to remain true to his mother and the Church, and to love and marry Capitú. The first part of this wish is made doubly clear by Santiago's stated wish in the few sentences immediately preceding the narration of the dream, of which the gist is: if it had not been for Capitú, he could have been a parish priest, a bishop, or even Pope.

> . . . as Uncle Cosme charged me: "Get along lad, and come back to me a Pope!" Ah! why did I not accomplish that wish? After Napoleon, lieuten-

ant and emperor, all destinies are possible in this world.

As for the dream, it was this.

The dream, as it stands, with its obvious interpretation, runs as follows: he was looking for Capitú's lovers and he saw one (that is, he wanted her to be untrue to him and she was, with the implied consequence that now he would abandon her and remain true to his mother and God). Then the contrary wish: the lover ran away—did not exist (that is, he would love Capitú). Then the first wish again: her father was weeping over the lottery ticket which had come out a blank. (We already know that this signified to Bento his entering the priesthood and not marrying Capitú, for when Padua said good-bye to Bento on the eve of his departure for the seminary, "his eyes were moist in earnest. His face wore a disenchanted look like a man who has spent his whole hoard of hopes on a single lottery ticket and sees the accursed number come out a blank—such a sweet number!") Then the contrary wish, stated completely and unequivocably this time: Capitú promised him the "grand prize" with her eyes and lips, Padua and his ticket disappeared, the street was deserted of lovers, Capitú leaned out the window of her house, Bento took her hands.

For the old Dom Casmurro the dream contains the same wish as the sonnet and the house—to return to his adolescence—only it appears with a slight change: would that the beginning of his life had contained the Casmurro element—his jealousy and his regrets at abandoning the Church and his mother—and the last part of his life the sweet, self-abandoned Bento-Capitú element. In other words, instead of resurrecting his dead soul, his ability to love—something he had found impossible—here the wish is to begin with the bad predominating, that is with little or no soul, let the bad die and the soul come forth like a butterfly from a cocoon. In this wish, Santiago identifies the soul, the good, with Capitú and his love of her.

This wish is stated more succinctly in the first of the two chapters that logically follow and explain the dream, "A dramatic reform," in which he advocates that a tragedy should begin with the tragic outcome and go backwards to end with a happy beginning. He illustrates his advocated reform with *Othello,* which he tells us later was *his* tragedy—except that his Desdemona was guilty.

The dream can be interpreted in a third way. Like the number on Padua's lottery ticket, 4004, it may be read either forward or backward. (And of course logical and chronological order in dreams is not infrequently reversed.) If we start with the last wish and go backwards to the beginning, the dream becomes prophetic: Capitú gave Bento her love which promised the "grand prize" of perfect love and conjugal felicity. This idea is reinforced by the perfectness of the number on Padua's lottery ticket, for there is evidence that Bento identified himself with Padua:[17] that is to say, destiny promised Padua (Bento) the "grand prize" but "the wheel of destiny broke down" (Santiago's ability to love broke down), and he ended spying out Capitú's phantom lover(s)—and *Othello* began and ended as Shakespeare, destiny's "plagiarist," intended.

Pandora-Nature-Destiny

The second of these two chapters, "The stage manager," continues the symbolism of life as a dramatic struggle—in the "sonnet" chapter it was a battle between heaven and earth. The author-stage manager of the piece is destiny. What was "destiny" to Santiago and to Machado de Assis? To Machado de Assis it was "Pandora," "nature," "life including death," "good including evil."[18] Even in *Dom Casmurro* we

104

find these other terms "Pandora" and "nature" used for "destiny." Pandora gave Santiago's father and mother a lucky ticket, but Santiago a blank[19]—which means nature formed them for happiness, him for unhappiness. Fortune changed places with nature in the writing of Uncle Cosme's life drama[20]—which is only a way of saying that Cosme's virtues were not strong enough to combat adversity. Nature made Santiago a "flower"—but one like Cosme, that withered and died. She made Capitú a flower—an everlasting. Destiny introduced Escobar into the drama;[21] destiny planted the "letter" Ezekiel.[22] That is, Bento Santiago's nature—his good and evil geniuses—wrote the parts Escobar, Ezekiel, Capitú, and the others were to play in his life drama.[23]

The Opera

To an Italian tenor, naturally, the only form of drama is an opera. Santiago "accepted Marcolini's definition": his life was an opera in which the words written by God fought with the music written by Satan. Exactly how did Santiago apply this allegory to his own life? The opera to him was apparently the early Christian ascetic's struggle between soul and body—in which he identified himself and his pious mother with the libretto of God, and Capitú and her vulgar father and mother with the devil's music. It was not till he became conscious of his love for Capitú that he knew he "had already begun to sing" the devil's music.[24] In relating the second kiss, Santiago comments: "I knew nothing of the Scriptures. If I had, it is probable that the spirit of Satan would have prompted me to give the language of the Canticles a direct and natural signification." Here is something of a twist: the spirit of Satan coming out of Holy Writ. But we must always keep in mind that we are considering Santiago's interpretation of the "Opera," not Machado de Assis's. In chapter lviii ("The treaty") Santiago confesses his adolescent sexual interest in girls, and again identifies it with the temptation of Satan. When Bento wished his mother dead that he might be free to love Capitú, "it was the prompting of lust and selfishness."[25] In chapter xcvii ("The sallying forth") he again adverts to his interest in other girls, with the same implication: "Though a son of the seminary and my mother, I had already begun to feel beneath my chaste restraint twitches of immodesty and boldness. They came from the blood . . . and vanity." After he ogled Sancha and squeezed her hand, the devil's seconds got intercalated into the minutes of God.[26]

In other words, love for Capitú and passing fancies are not differentiated: love to Santiago, as to Iago, "is merely a lust of the blood and a permission of the will"—the spirit of Satan. Only his love for his mother is of God. But he is not completely consistent in his use of these symbols. The young Bento at times identified Capitú with the holiness surrounding himself and his mother: for example, when he first realized he loved Capitú.

> I, future padre, thus stood before her as before an altar, and one side of her face was the Epistle and the other the Gospel. Her mouth the chalice, her lips the paten . . . We stood there with heaven in us. Our hands united our nerves, and made of two creatures one—and that one a seraph.[27]

When he felt himself drawn into the great tide of her love, Santiago remarks, "Only the clocks of heaven will have noted this space of time which was infinite yet brief."[28] In the reconciliation after the first quarrel, Bento "felt [his] eyes grow moist . . . It was pure love."[29] Again: Santiago's apostrophe to Capitú on the occasion of Bento's departure for the seminary—

> O sweet companion of my childish days, I was pure, pure I remained and pure I entered the

halls of São José to seek in appearance, the sacerdotal investiture; and before it, the *call*. But the *call* was you, the investiture was you.[30]

Then follows Bento's momentary consideration of Capitú as the "flower of heaven," and the other references to her as a "flower," and the reference to her as "the angel of the Scriptures."

In chapter lxxx ("Let us enter the chapter") Santiago's confusion of symbols is made manifest by his interpretation of his mother's feelings.

> Little by little my mother was persuaded that this girl would make me happy. Then, finally, hope that our love, rendering me absolutely intolerant of the seminary, would make me refuse to stay there either for God or the devil: this secret hope began to invade my mother's heart.

Who is the devil and who is God now? As far as Bento was concerned, José Dias's fanciful description of a trip to Rome and absolution by the Pope, with the Virgin Mary, Jesus, and choirs of angels singing hosannahs[31] was as good as a direct blessing from God on marriage to Capitú, and prepared for that marriage "in heaven," attended by God's blessing in the form of good-omened rain, heavenly candles, St. Peter's welcome, choiring angels, and so on.[32]

Numbers

In spite of these inconsistencies in Santiago's interpretation of the allegory of his life, he manages to leave the reader with the impression that he is of God, and Capitú of the devil and deceitful to the core. To return to his remark at the conclusion of Marcolini's "opera," ". . . my life fits his definition. I sang a tender *duo,* then a *trio,* then a *quatuor.*"

Santiago, it would seem, interprets the other members of the devil's quartet as Capitú, Escobar, and Ezekiel. There is particularly no doubt about Escobar: he was the "terceiro" ("go-between") between Capitú and Bento for their letters;[33] he was the "terceiro" ("third party") in "Third party claim proceeding."[34] (Yet there is perhaps more reason to believe that it was Casmurro who came between Bento and Capitú as an inharmonious "terceiro.") In "The hand of Sancha," with Escobar's secret project "for the four of us," and Santiago's "contradança," the quartet becomes Santiago, Capitú, Sancha, and Escobar. Though Santiago tosses the symbol "four" about in this way, it is still fairly clear that he would have us interpret his quartet as Bento, Capitú, Escobar, and Ezekiel: when friends asked if he was going to make an oration at Escobar's funeral his reply was, yes, he would say "four" words.[35]

But what of the mystic number on the dream lottery ticket, 4004? If we wish to go beyond the simple interpretation as indicated above, we should, I believe, consult the chapter "Arithmetical ideas," in which Escobar, who was an "arithmetical head $(2 + 2 = 4)$," explained the beauty of mathematics to his young classmate.

> "Look at the digits: there are no two which perform the same function: 4 is 4, and 7 is 7. And consider the beauty with which a 4 and a 7 form this thing which is represented by 11. Now double 11 and you have 22. Multiply it by itself, it makes 484, and so on. But where the perfection is greatest is in the use of *zero*. The value of *zero* is, in itself, nothing; but what is the function of this negative symbol?—to augment! A 5 alone is a 5: place 00 with it, it is 500. Thus, that which has no value makes great value . . ."

Is this not what Santiago did?—placed after the 4 (Santiago, Capitú, Escobar, and Ezekiel) "nothing" followed by the same 4, to make the powerful number 4004? Whatever the correct interpretation is, I am willing to believe that Machado de Assis loaded both

4 and 4004 with multiple symbolism, just as he loaded a word with multiple meaning. I am willing to believe that the other figures in this chapter on arithmetical ideas have their significance—in particular Dona Gloria's "nine houses" with their income of "1:070$000." I believe, further, that this chapter explains the *ten* in Capitú's "ten pounds sterling."[36] As Escobar explained, no matter how great and beautiful a mathematical display may be, there are only ten digits— they are the basis of everything. Machado was familiar with the figurative meaning of the word "sterling," as we have noted above. When Capitú gave Santiago her ten pounds sterling, she did the same thing that Dona Gloria of the portrait did in offering the flower to her portrait-husband: " 'I am all yours, my gallant cavalier,' " and Santiago's momentary reaction was the same as his father's, " 'See how the girl loves me!' "

Of course, the ten pounds sterling has another implication—a literal one—of Bento Santiago's interest in money; and this no doubt was what caused Escobar to stare in amazement.

To come back to the digit 4, and 4004, there are still other significant "fours" in Santiago's story: the "four seasons" in his "house," the "four busts painted on the walls," his "madness-and-sin" "virtue-and-reason"—a kind of doubling of God and the devil, love and hate, or Bento and Casmurro. (It is only natural that the twofold Santiago [Bento-Casmurro] should see double.) But before going into Santiago's "married couples," let us briefly consider a recurring symbol peculiarly attached to Capitú, and a few secondary ones, which shed light on this matter of the "married couples."

The Sea

As mentioned above, Machado de Assis was familiar with the Greek myth that the goddess of love was born of the sea. And we have seen that Santiago was afraid of losing himself in the tide of Capitú's eyes. In that same chapter he compares her to Thetis, which is what Camões calls Tethys—the sea—daughter of Heaven and Earth, who surrounded Adamastor (lust and self-love) with the waves of her love. Even in this early chapter, Santiago tells us Capitú's love embraced all the potencies both Christian and pagan. And we saw that Capitú, in her jealous fear of Dona Gloria, would have sent Bento over the sea of her love out of Gloria's reach. When Bento, on Capitú's instructions, was trying to convert José Dias to their plan, he gazed out to sea.[37] The first quarrel, as the later ones, are likened to storms at sea.[38] The young couple went to live on the sea (Gloria Beach), and spent their nights gazing at the sea and sky.[39] Santiago was jealous of Capitú's contemplation of the sea.[40] After Ezekiel was born, Escobar and Santiago would go down to the beach or to the Passeio Público (from which could be seen the sea).[41] Escobar moved to a house on the sea, and the two couples passed their evenings in Santiago's or Escobar's house, "gazing at the sea."[42] When Bento and Sancha made love, the sea was angry.[43] Escobar had lungs and arms to swim in the sea,[44] but he went too far and drowned in the sea[45]—and *this* sea is identified with Capitú's eyes.[46] When Santiago decided to commit suicide, that is, to separate himself from Capitú and her love, he thought, "I would never again contemplate the sea beyond Gloria."[47] He compares the loss of his love for Capitú to shipwreck: ". . . though I have always been a landsman, I tell this part of my life as an old sailor recalls his shipwreck."[48] Long after Escobar's death, he tells us, he went to Escobar's house on the beach,

> to test if the old sensations were dead or merely sleeping. I cannot quite tell because sleep, when it is heavy, confounds the living with the dead, except that the living breathe. I *was* breathing,

but (perhaps because of the sea) with some difficulty.[49]

In these last similes we again come upon the seed of the tragedy—it is the same as in *Resurreição*. The Bento in Santiago was weak; his capacity for love was weak, he was a "landsman," and did not have "lungs" or "muscles" for swimming in the sea.

Thus the implication of the "sea" symbol, as far as Santiago is concerned, is the same as that of the house, the sonnet, and the dream: failure; shipwreck; loss of soul, of heaven, life, love.

Colors, Trees, Birds

And Capitú? It is not only the flower and the sea that identify Capitú with love, life, spirituality. There is the color blue. In Machadean terminology "blue," "blue sky," "sun and blue sky," are also love, life, and love's faith. And this symbol is connected with Capitú, who was "the sun," "sunshine and blue sky,"[50] with the young Bento and the young Escobar, and the dying José Dias, for all of whom "the sky was blue."[51] But the color yellow, which symbolizes jealousy, is associated with the later Santiago—Santiago Casmurro —though he tries to escape it on the wings of a lacuna.

> My memory is not good . . . How I envy those who have not forgotten the color of their first trousers! *I* am not sure of the color of those I put on yesterday. I can only swear they were not yellow, because I detest that color—but even this may be forgetfulness and confusion. And rather forgetfulness than confusion.[52]

The trees, which touch the blue sky, are thoughts —but of a certain type—happy, free, bold, timeless ideas infused with life, love, God: the old coconut palm that approved of young love,[53] the palm tossing against the sky and breathing life,[54] the trees on the Matacavallos place, which knew Bento but did not recognize Casmurro.[55]

111

The birds which hide in the trees are also thoughts, but of a quite different sort: they are limited thoughts, shrewd thoughts, sad thoughts, memories and regrets, thoughts that die with time, death.[56] The flowers painted on the wall of Dom Casmurro's reconstructed house were supported by "sturdy birds"—and his love was only a memory maintained by "comparison and reflection."[57] The same imagery applies to the original house: at the beginning of the narrative Dona Gloria's love was likewise little more than a memory—the cult of a portrait, and a tomb in the nearby church; and her son was to be entombed also. It was not until Capitú became "the flower of the house, the sun of its mornings, the moon of its nights, the cool of its evenings," that Dona Gloria's "flower" lived again.[58]

When the young Santiago, in order to temporize with a bad situation, was trying to outwit José Dias in the Passeio Público, the sinuous movements of his thoughts were mirrored by "the fantastic dances of big, dark birds" on the shore below. (It may be noted too that the sky was half-clouded over in this scene.)[59]

Padua's little caged birds—which sounded like all the devils of hell to Bento—reflect his harmless, vulgar ambitions and vainglory.[60]

The swallows flying back and forth during the early quarrel scene between Bento and Capitú, represent their "regrets" and "memories"—that is, in Santiago's interpretation, part of their love had already died.[61] And the "treading swallows" are identified with his coarse suspicions of Capitú and Escobar.[62]

Finally there is that dark, ugly bird beating its wings in Santiago's brain—death itself, which has to "come to life" in order to exist.[63]

Even with these minor symbols, the message is the same. Bento was love and life, though Casmurro was present even in the young Santiago who was hugged by death (when he imagined and wished his mother dead).[64] Dom Casmurro had death in his brain and death in the pocket of his yellow trousers. But Capitú was "the opposite of death."[65]

The Married Couple

The struggle of the "married couple" is the same drama as the "opera" with the same playwright-producer who goes under the name of nature instead of God:

> Each person is born with a certain number of sins and virtues allied by matrimony to compensate each other in life, when one of these consorts is stronger than the other it alone guides the individual.[66]

Santiago makes no direct reference to anyone's "married couple" but his own. In Capitú's case there is even little indirect evidence of much of a struggle between her "consorts." As the sea symbolism demonstrates, she is an image of self-abandoned love. Her early jealousy of Dona Gloria and Sancha, her ambition, fondness for pleasure and luxury, vanity, even intellect, were quickly conquered and made subservient to her spiritual beauty—her love. Soon after he entered the seminary Santiago found in her "a new imperium":[67] love had taken command. Her love embraced not only Bento, but even Casmurro, Dona Gloria, José Dias, Justina, and the others. All these personages felt the force of it; the struggle between their "consorts" was affected by it. Justina, though her acrimonious consort no doubt continued to govern her to the end of her days, was "captivated," and softened, and finally lost her bitter tongue.[68] The flower in the selfish, superstitious, vain, acquisitive, domineering Gloria was brought to life. The most notable example is José Dias, who first appears as a petty contriver for self-interest, an "Iago," and a "trouble-maker"; but his own interests gave way before his devotion to the Santiagos and Capitú. His final wish was to see "the blue sky"—which identifies him definitely with good, life, and love. His struggle began with evil holding the upper hand and ended with the triumph of good. Santiago's story was the reverse. The young Bento was predominantly good, nature made him the son of a good woman who gave a great love to the good man who was Bento's father, a woman who loved her son, was kind to her relatives and dependents, who loved God.

But this was not all Bento Santiago inherited. When the story opens, Dona Gloria's love was a kind of dead thing: it had partly died with her husband, perhaps even before, as Santiago intimates,[69] and her pre-occupation was with money and the domination of the lives of others. When she sold the plantation she sold most of the slaves along with it, she bought new slaves, many of whom she sent into the streets to earn her money by shining shoes, peddling, portering and the like. This was a reprehensible practice in Brazil, as Simon Legree's operations were in the United States. She made herself "old" deliberately (though "nature tried to preserve her from the action of time"), by supervising the work of the slaves at home. She engaged in real estate deals and other profitable investments. And what did she do with her money? She gave a few "coppers" to José Dias from time to time, gave her poor brother an ambling mount to go to work on when it was apparent his weight and bad heart really required a carriage, on rare occasions invited Cabral to dinner, sent a bunch of flowers to put on the corpse of Manduca. But the crowning example of her selfishness was her plan to make a priest of her son in order to keep him for herself.

She talked piety, displayed a certain amount of superstitious fear, but evidence of Christian charity in her acts is rather slim. Her vanity is indicated by the friends she had about her—two dependent relatives, Padre Cabral, Dr. João da Costa, the Paduas—all inferior to her in social position, money, and brains—who took her advice, "yesed" her, and showered her with adulation. And she permitted them to liken her to the Virgin Mary. A touch of snobbery is indicated by her exclusiveness ("The old chaise") and by her refusal to allow Bento to attend Manduca's funeral.

In addition to the lingering fragrance of her love for her husband, and her gentle manners, she had one other great redeeming virtue: an ingenuousness (except in money matters), a tendency to trust and believe in the good motives of others. This was the "window" through which Capitú's love entered and resurrected Dona Gloria's soul.

Santiago was the son of his mother, as he himself states, but he inherited from Cosme and Justina also —from the one his detachment, his gluttony, and his general concern with physical comfort; from the other, her envy and cynicism, her tendency to suspect the motives of others. And his character was no doubt affected by the envy, jealousy, hypocrisy, and deviousness of the early José Dias, the obsequiousness and vanity of Cabral, the servility of the slaves, and by the naturalness and warmth of the Paduas, and the faith of Manduca.

It is Santiago himself who identifies his good and evil consorts as the loving, ingenuous, Christian Bento, and the detached, suspicious, nonbelieving Casmurro; it is he who tells us that Bento became Casmurro, and also that Casmurro was in Bento and finally emerged from Bento. For most of the story it is Bento who acts; Casmurro manifests himself as "velleities," vague wishes, sometimes not so vague—as a desire to say a bad word to Padre Cabral, to kick José Dias into the street, to shake him, to torture his mother by telling her he no longer loves her but only Capitú, by a desire to shake Capitú, to sink his nails into her throat and watch the blood ebb from her with her life, a wish to see his mother dead, to kill Cousin Justina. Finally Casmurro threw off the domination of Bento and emerged as a man of action.[70] From then on the roles are reversed, for the most part; it is Casmurro who acts and Bento who wishes and reminisces.

But from the start Bento and Casmurro are two personalities warring with each other. The ferocity of this struggle and the strength of Casmurro are indicated in the description of Santiago's second attack of jealousy.

> I did not escape myself. I ran to my room and entered behind myself. I talked to myself, persecuted myself, threw myself on the bed and rolled over and over with myself . . . As I lay on the bed I heard [Capitú's] voice . . . I continued alone with myself . . .[71]

The above quotation indicates a struggle and the presence of two persons. What I have omitted from this passage shows the true nature of Casmurro. Let us restore the omissions.

> I swore I would not visit Capitú that afternoon, nor ever again, and that I would become a padre straight off.

> I saw myself already ordained, standing before her. She wept repentantly and begged my forgiveness, but I, cold and serene, had nothing but scorn, scorn and contempt. I turned my back on her and called her perverse.

> Twice I found myself gnashing my teeth, as if I had her between them . . . I continued deaf, alone with myself and my scorn. And I was filled with a desire to drive my nails into her throat, bury them deep, and watch the life drain out of her with her blood . . .

In other words Casmurro is hatred and revenge. We see, further, that the priesthood which Santiago elsewhere has associated with his mother, God, and the libretto of God, is no such thing: it is only the opposite of love; it is watching Capitú's life drain out of her; it is cold murder and revenge.[72]

When the "new man of action" Casmurro emerged

from Santiago he put this wish into execution: he rejected Capitú's love, refused her his, sent her away, and lived as a recluse.[73] But, note, there was nothing godly about that cloister in Engenho Novo, there was no repentance, he ate well, slept well, went to the theater, had mistresses and gay companions, went on hating Ezekiel, José Dias, the dead Escobar, Capitú, even his mother, with a cold, detached hatred—alone with his scorn and contempt.

So changed was this new Casmurro-dominated man from the old married couple in which Bento dominated, that destiny's "grand prize," to him, represented "death": "When I found myself with death in my pocket I felt as if I had just drawn the grand prize— no, greater joy; for a lottery prize dribbles away, but death does not."[74] Love, for him, had "dribbled away." Once more we touch on the real cause of Santiago's tragedy: his ability to love was subject to death. *Dom Casmurro* is essentially the same story as *Resurreição*.

When Felix, the hero of that novel, told Livia he had "embraced a serpent," he spoke the truth but not as he meant it: he had embraced death. Death, you will recall, also embraced Bento. And death in the form of jealousy sank its "fang" into him. No matter how often his love was resurrected, death struck again,[75] for death did not dribble away. Time, "death's minister,"[76] blotted out his "longings and resurrections" of Manduca;[77] time destroyed the "pyramids" and the "air castles" (Bento's love for Capitú and Escobar).[78]

Note the relationship between life and death; it is the same as that between good and evil, God and the devil. These pairs are each in conflict. But the devil along with the "theater and performers" of Marcolini's "opera" were all created by God, or, as the Manduca episode illustrated, "God writes straight with crooked lines." Evil is a part of good. Death is a part of life—as Santiago states in two different places in his narrative. His comment on the bird of death, which beat its wings in an effort to get out of his brain, is: "Life is so beautiful that even the idea of death must come to life in order to exist." And, after recording José Dias's final superlative, when the dying man looked at the blue sky and said "most beautiful," Santiago adds: "His last superlative . . . made death a fragment of life."

9

Othello's Tears

THE CONCEPT that death is a part of life, evil of good, is not peculiar to *Dom Casmurro*. It is found elsewhere in Machado de Assis.[1] But it is this concept which explains his adaptation of Shakespeare's *Othello* in *Dom Casmurro*. To reword our symbolism, "destiny, the playwright-producer," in the shape of the "plagiarist" Machado de Assis, has presented an *Othello*—an altered *Othello*, but not altered in either of the ways suggested by Santiago. He neither created a guilty Desdemona nor began the play at the end. He simply placed the opposite natures Iago and Othello in one man. There is nothing particularly novel in this. Shakespeare himself did it in *The Winter's Tale*. And, as mentioned above, many scholars have regarded Iago as a symbol of the evil in Othello, and in all men; others go so far as to argue that *Othello* is basically a mystery play with Desdemona representing Christ, Iago, the devil, and Othello, man. This interpretation, too, fits *Dom Casmurro* but with a paradoxical twist, as one might expect of Machado de Assis.

Santiago, as we have seen, associated Capitú with Satan, and himself with Christ. He also, by his allusions, associated her love with Venus and Tethys, pagan deities, and with the Roman heroine Lucretia. He pointed up her admiration for Julius Caesar, her desire to learn Latin—to Bento the language of Pontius Pilate, brought under control by the rules of Padre Pereira's grammar[2] —and he questioned her piety. In the same way, he associated Manduca with the devil, hog manure, and the heathen Turks, whereas Bento was nature's sweet violet, flower of heaven, and on the side of the Christian Russians. The symbolism of the book as a whole, however, told us a different story.

Machado also associates Capitú with the pagans, by her name, and by so doing her love is made the more Christian. For Machado de Assis did not regard "seminaries," the "Church," even "prayers," or other outward manifestations and ceremony as necessarily identical with the spirit of Christ. To him love was love, no matter what you call it. One may compare the converted Jewess of his poem "A Cristã Nova," who in order to be truly Christlike lies and says she is a Jew.[3] As Machado's created author Ayres writes in *Esaú e Jacob,* "God is God, and if a Mohammedan girl is reading me let her read 'Allah' in place of 'God.' "[4] His point is that the spirit of Christ existed before and outside Christ, that love engenders pity, courage, devotion, faith, and all the other Christian virtues. Capitú's love, though great and beautiful, at the beginning contained some dross, as we have seen, of vanity, jealousy, and selfish ambition; but love fostered in her the spirit of Christ. At the end of the book, it is Capitú, not Santiago with his multitudinous prayers, who embodies Christian charity ("caridade"): she spared Dona Gloria and the others, brought up her son to love and admire his father—these acts constitute a lie, but like the converted Jewess' lie and Desdemona's deathbed lie, it is Christlike—and she herself continued to write Santiago loving letters. She had no bitterness. Her "flower" may have been "pale and solitary" but there was no worm at the heart of it. It is Santiago who was the unbeliever; he laughed at her Christianity, as Othello scoffed at Desdemona's. Capitú summed up the truth in her last words: "You, in spite of the seminary, do not believe in God. I believe."[5]

To revert once more to the symbolism of Capitú's name: Machado de Assis's poem "Visão"[6] explains how the Capitolium, originally the home of the "Roman eagle" ("force and power"), is now the home of "Christ's dove" ("love"). This is what happened in Capitú's case: her "eagle" gave way to "the dove." Thus the paradox disappears, but in another sense it remains.

Machado de Assis believed that human nature did not, on the whole, change very fast, nor without struggle and setbacks. As he remarks in one of his columns, "civilization is not an easy jaunt."[7] The context of this quotation indicates that he did not believe civilization always marched forward, sometimes it went backward or around in circles. Thus one does not find in his writings a great deal in the way of smug satisfaction with his own century and country; and some of his critics have taken this lack as a sign of a deep-rooted pessimism; however, one finds him looking forward to the next century with hope,[8] and hope is not usually associated with pessimism. But it was his own age and country he mirrored and criticized in his fiction. For it was only through knowledge of self, he believed, that human beings could, with purpose and effort, improve. Thus, we find running through his works, almost as a motif, the idea that the restraints imposed by nineteenth-century Brazilian society, with its tradition of Christian-Catholic devotion and what passed for Christian piety, did not lessen the strength of human passion but only altered its manifestation—and the new manifestation was not necessarily more acceptable than the old.

When he was twenty-five years old, for example, he took issue, in his weekly column in the *Diário do Rio de Janeiro*, with a Catholic journal of Paris *Le Monde* for its attitude on capital punishment—which Machado de Assis thought should be abolished, to have done with the anomaly of maintaining a law of blood which was responsible for sacrificing the founder of the religious base of modern societies . . . But [*Le Monde*] is against the guillotine as being an invention of the Revolution; it is for having some other death penalty of Catholic invention. Burning perhaps?

[*Le Monde*] is of the opinion that it is an impious act to kill with the guillotine; what it wants is for the killing to be done in a more Catholic, a more pious manner, with an instrument sanctioned by clerical tradition and not with one of Revolutionary invention. For [*Le Monde*] the question is simply one of form; the basic principle must be maintained and respected.[9]

This feeling is expressed artistically in the short story "Entre Santos," in which Christian saints come down from their altars and indulge in a cruel mirth at the expense of their worshipers. "And the saints laughed, not with the great rowdy guffaw of Homer's gods when they saw the lame Vulcan serving at table, but with a laugh that was modest, self-contained, beatific, and Catholic."

In both instances one observes primitive, natural, pagan brutality set over against modern, refined, Christian-Catholic cruelty. Christian is used as a synonym for "repression," with all it may imply in the way of hypocrisy and calculation, and pagan has become a synonym for "naturalness," "spontaneity," "ingenuousness."

In *Dom Casmurro*, Bento is identified with Christianity by his name, by his mother's vow, by his upbringing, his prayers, his display of devotion, and so on; he even tries to sublimate his honeymoon into a mystical and heavenly rite. But we must also consider the attitude in which we first find him, eavesdropping behind a door; and we must consider that other time we find him hiding behind a door—after he has delivered the eulogy at Escobar's funeral. His situation, he tells us, was worse than that of Priam who kissed the hand of his son's murderer, yet he, Santiago, did not weep and tear his hair because the tears of modern-day Priams "are wiped away behind the door so that their faces may appear bright and clean. Their talk is rather of joy than of melancholy, and all goes along as if Achilles had not slain Hector."[10]

Yet we are to learn that all *does not* go along as if Achilles had not slain Hector. For all the tears are wiped away, the passion remains in his heart, tough, resistant, terrible. Our repressed, *Christian* Priam exacts his own; the ancient Priam forgave his son's murderer. Our modern Priam demands a more cruel revenge than the savage Achilles wreaked on Hector. This is Machado's paradox. Capitú's love for being pagan—natural, spontaneous, unrepressed—is the more pure, the more Christian. Santiago's repression turns his love to un-Christian self-love, wounded vanity, lust, and hate. In *Resurreição* Machado de Assis states plainly what love should be and should not be: "[Felix's] nature had two sides . . . one natural and spontaneous, the other calculating and deliberate."[11]

Machado de Assis extended the meaning embodied in "pagan" to include the resurrected paganism, the Renaissance passions as found in Shakespeare's plays. It became, one might say, his favorite sport to turn Shakespeare's characters loose on the shores of Guanabara Bay and observe their antics. I will cite one example, which clearly demonstrates what he believed happened to Renaissance passion when it was subjected to the Portuguese-Christian-Catholic influence of nineteenth-century Brazil.

In his last novel (*Memorial de Ayres*), not only did Machado de Assis attempt a multiple plot in the manner of Shakespeare, but one of the plots is the story of a Brazilian Juliet and her Romeo. Old Ayres, the narrator of the novel, refers to them as such, and to their respective fathers, who were political enemies, as "Capulet" and "Montague." There is the love at first sight, occurring at the theater. There follow the tyrannical actions of Baron Santa Pia (Capulet), who "preferred to see his daughter dead at his feet, or mad, rather than have his blood mixed with that of the Noronhas (Montagues)." "Lady Capulet" at first sided with her husband. Fidelia (Juliet), locked in her room, wept endlessly and staged a hunger strike while the servants sympathized. Campos, Baron Santa Pia's brother, like Prince Escalus of Verona, tried to conciliate the two families, et cetera, et cetera. But the outcome was quite different from that of *Romeo and Juliet* because the passions of the principals did not burst into short-lived violence. In this instance, Lady Capulet, concerned for her daughter's health, persuaded her lord to allow his daughter to marry her Romeo. He did, but with a command never to darken his door again. Eduardo (Romeo) was likewise disowned by his father. The happiness of the young couple was brief, however. Eduardo died, of natural causes, within a year. For three years Fidelia daily tended the grave of her Romeo. For seven years she and her father, and her father-in-law, remained estranged, till old Santa-Pia Capulet lay on his death bed, still adamant in his political convictions, recalcitrant against the orders of the state (on emancipation), and unrelenting toward his daughter, the dead Romeo, and old Montague; and so he died, with only a vague gesture of forgiveness toward Fidelia, though Campos (Prince Escalus) had been trying all the while to bring about a reconciliation. Immediately after her father's funeral, this sweet, but pigheaded, Rio Juliet had his portrait and her dead Romeo's placed in matching frames over her mantel. As she explained to Ayres, ". . . now that death had reconciled them she wished to reconcile them in effigy." And Ayres sarcastically prophesies: "Five years from now she'll have her father's bones transferred to her husband's tomb and she'll reconcile them in the earth in as much as eternity has already reconciled them."[12]

In this story the polite, but tough, persistent passion of refined, Christian, nineteenth-century Brazilians, descended from Portuguese conquerors, resulted in comedy. In Santiago's case the result was tragedy.

Santiago's jealousy of Capitú first broke forth when he was fifteen years old—when he had a desire to sink his nails into her throat and watch her blood drain out of her with her life. But he waited fifteen years to wreak his revenge, which was then without bloodshed, a revenge that was "modest, self-contained, beatific, and Catholic," a civilized, nineteenth-century revenge many times more cruel than Othello's. Santiago's passion, though as intense as Othello's did not explode in a blinding shower of flames: it smoldered with a slow, indestructible heat that shriveled and hardened the generous part of his nature until there was scarcely a trace of Bento left, and he was all Casmurro. Othello's jealousy turned him into a Moor; Bento's turned him into a "casmurro." For, I believe, Machado de Assis punned on this word: the English word "Moor" and the middle syllable of "casmurro" have practically the same sound. To any one who enjoyed playing upon words as Machado de Assis did, such a pun would not be at all impossible—on the contrary, it would be irresistible, and in so doing he had no less a model than Shakespeare himself, who punned on the word "Moor" "more" than once.[13]

Santiago's tragedy, like Macbeth's or Othello's, proceeded from a flaw in an otherwise noble nature; but his fall was different. Othello's soul went clanging down to hell, where, perhaps, it would be redeemed by the goodness of Desdemona and his love for her. Bento Santiago did not die but, like Sophocles' Oedipus, suffered "a kind of obliteration, a severance from his own past life and from the lives of other men"[14]—he became "casmurro." Thus the catastrophe of *Dom Casmurro* is not Shakespearean but Sophoclean.

This kind of multiple "plagiarism" was a part of Machado de Assis's artistic creed and practice. As he wrote in one of his columns:

> I know that history does not repeat itself. The French Revolution and *Othello* have been written; still there is nothing to prevent one from lifting this or that scene and using it in other dramas: thus are committed, literarily speaking, acts of plagiarism.[15]

Machado de Assis did not limit his "lifting" to Shakespeare and the Greeks, nor yet to the French Revolution. For *Dom Casmurro* alone he drew heavily on Montaigne and the Bible, and borrowed touches from Fielding, Sterne, and other authors; but none of these borrowings has the significance of the Shakespearean element, which is essential.

10

Shakespeare under the
Southern Cross

SANTIAGO'S FINAL CHAPTER, which has been compared
to a lawyer's summation for the jury, also calls to mind
Othello's speech—

Soft you; a word or two before you go.
I have done the state some service, and
   they know't;
No more of that. I pray you, in your letters,
When you shall these unlucky deeds relate,
Speak of me as I am; nothing extenuate,
Nor set down aught in malice: then, must
   you speak
Of one that lov'd not wisely but too well;
Of one not easily jealous, but being wrought,
Perplex'd in the extreme . . .

From there on, of course, any analogy ceases: Santiago
did not repent nor admit error.

But there is another, perhaps more meaningful, allusion in this last chapter—in its title "Well and the
rest" and in the play on the words "resto" and "restar."
What connotation clung to the phrase "o resto" in
Santiago's mind, we can only guess; for Machado de
Assis, old Shakespeare-lover that he was, there is not
much room for doubt: he played on the phrase too
often: "o resto é certo,"[1] "o resto é sabido,"[2] "o resto

está em Victor Hugo,"[3] "o *resto é relativo*,"[4] "the rest is silence"[5]—Hamlet's four, final, mysterious words to Horatio.

The fact that with Santiago the rest is *not* "silence" does not lessen the force of the allusion. Neither does the fact that Santiago defines "the rest" in terms of Capitú, though at first glance it may seem to. "The rest," according to Santiago, is that the earlier deceitful Capitú was in the later deceitful Capitú like the fruit within its rind, that the green fruit matured, or, to put it more literally, that her deceit grew and culminated in crime. If this is "the rest," the story has been an account of Capitú's betrayal of the loving Bento and should have been titled *Capitú* or *Eyes Like the Tide* or *The Sly Gypsy*. But the title is *Dom Casmurro*, and rightly so.

To return to the allusion. Hamlet was a man in whom the forces of brutality, hate, and suspicion struggled against the forces of gentleness and love, with brutality and hate, at least temporarily, winning out. Let us apply Santiago's definition of "the rest" to himself: Dom Casmurro was within Bento like a rottenness at the core of a fair fruit; the rottenness grew until it came through the rind. Santiago uses such a metaphor in describing his sudden change to a man of action: "Could it be that there was a strange man within me, a man who now began to show himself as the result of new, strong pressures? If so, it was a man scarcely hidden beneath the surface."[6]

Santiago not only tells of the emergence of the man of cruel action from within himself, he refers directly to the change from Bento to Dom Casmurro on a number of occasions.[7] And in his first two chapters, which chronologically follow all the others, he states that he is Dom Casmurro, gives his own softened interpretation of the epithet, and, further, provides us with a clear illustration of what "casmurro" really means. He displays his detachment, cynical distrust, and coldness

128

to all human affection—by his remark about his young poet-neighbor, "with a little effort, since the title is his, he will be able to decide that the work is his"; by his sarcastic wit at the expense of his old friends who have gone to study the geology of cemeteries and for whose loss he is "pretty much consoled"; by his contemptuous appraisal of his mistresses; by his offhand reference to the death of Bento, "I myself am missing . . . what is here may be likened to dye on hair and beard: it barely preserves the outer *habit*, as they say in autopsies." Though he has lost family and friends, and even his own better nature, he "eats well," and "does not sleep badly."

Early in the book he gives an illustration of his "married couple" of "sin and virtue"—brutal hate and loving kindness;[8] and he would have us understand that he remained a mixture of good and evil, with good guiding his actions and evil evincing itself only as idle wishes. But in the later chapter referred to above (cxl), it is "the submerged man" (that is, the evil wish) that takes over and goes into action. As Hamlet the poet-lover, became Hamlet the murderer, so the gentle Bento became "casmurro." Is not this "the rest"? By putting Iago and Othello in the same man, Machado de Assis made a Hamlet. Felix of *Ressurreição* is constructed on much the same formula. Lest either Machado or I seem to be mixing *Hamlet* and *Othello* in unwarranted fashion, I might mention that this is good current practice in Shakespearean circles.[9]

When did the Hyde-like Casmurro in Bento first rear his ugly head? It was, I believe, in the chapter entitled "Uma ponta de Iago." It might seem that the Iago referred to in the chapter title is José Dias, because it is his remark that Capitú was gay and carefree, waiting to hook one of the eligible young aristocrats of the neighborhood, which set off Bento's jealous rage. But we have already seen that José Dias was only an abortive Iago, and here he appears completely oblivious to the effect of his remark. It is Santiago who repeats the chance remark to himself, who analyzes it, gives it visual form, extends it, embroiders upon it. In short, it is Santiago who plays the role of Iago to himself and sends himself into a trance or fit resembling Othello's when he had been worked upon by Iago.

The Iago of the title, then, clearly refers to Santiago and the jealous suspicion within him. What of the word "ponta"? "Ponta" means "tip" or "point." A secondary meaning is "trace or touch," and perhaps this is the meaning intended in the present case. But "ponta," in its original meaning of "tip or point" is used euphemistically to replace "corno" ("horn," as of an animal or the devil), which according to Caldas Aulete, whose dictionary was used by Machado de Assis,[10] is "a term excluded from polite conversation." Machado himself so uses "ponta" in the novel which preceded *Dom Casmurro* where he describes the hero's attempt to seduce his friend's wife.

> You would almost think he was the devil trying to deceive the girl with his two great, God-given archangel's wings, when he suddenly put them in his pocket, whipped off his cap, and disclosed two fiend's horns ("pontas") sunk in his forehead.[11]

If "ponta" in this title means "horn," Santiago identifies his jealousy not only with Iago but also with the devil.

Shakespeare's Iago was identified with the forces of darkness; Iago himself recognized the connection.[12] And, as mentioned above, Iago is generally regarded as a personification of evil, and a number of scholars consider *Othello* a mystery play with Iago actually playing the part of the devil.

Iago is not alone, there are other Shakespearean characters in league with supernatural forces of evil: Macbeth, for example. And we find allusions to *Macbeth* in *Dom Casmurro*—allusions, and also the supernatural machinery. Again, the "plagiarism" is not simple. Santiago's "story" was set in motion by a quotation from Goethe's *Faust:* "Ah there, are you come again, restless shades?" This quotation, closely followed by the allegory of the "opera" with its colloquies in heaven between God and Satan, gives the impression that Santiago perhaps identified himself with Faust and felt he had sold his soul to the devil. His frequent talk of "mortgaging his soul" heightens the impression. That Machado de Assis associated these lines of Goethe with murder victims seems clear, not only from *Dom Casmurro,* but also from his citation of them as conclusion to certain satiric reflections on druggists who send customers to their reward by mistaking labels on bottles.[13] And that his imagination associated the Faust story with Shakespeare is evident from another journalistic column, in which he gives a specious report of an Italian opera impresario—an ex-seminarist—who sold his soul (in this case his company) to the devil, cheated his subscribers in Rio de Janeiro, repented and became a monk. The little satire concludes as follows:

> This story, which begins with a casual conversation in Rio de Janeiro and ends with the dizzy entrance into the monastery of the Mendicants; the pact with Satan, the repentance, the remorse, the rejection of money and power, there is in all this a whiff of Shakespeare, an aspect of tragedy. Is this not a subject to inspire our dramatic poets to something? Even now we can imagine the effect that some future Shakespeare will draw out of it. Changes of scene: Naples, Rio de Janeiro, Buenos-Aires; tarantellas and seguidillas; street song and Gregorian chant; Satan an impresario, an impresario a monk; the real and the supernatural. Ah! if the divine author of *Hamlet* could have read an account like this in a chronicle of the Middle Ages![14]

Here we find some of the same mixture as in *Dom Casmurro:* Rio de Janeiro, an ex-seminarist, Faust, opera, and Shakespeare.

To return to Macbeth, he too, in a sense, sold his soul to the devil; and he was haunted by at least one ghost. *Macbeth* is a study of evil through a study of murder. *Dom Casmurro* contains a thread of *Macbeth:* it too is a study of evil through a study of murder, even though no actual bloodshed is involved, and no blood punishment is meted out to the criminal. Let us take a look at its *Macbeth*—or rather *Faust-Macbeth* motif. *Macbeth* opens with the lines,

> 1. *Witch.* When shall we three meet again?
> In thunder, lightning, or in rain?
> 2. *Witch.* When the hurlyburly's done,
> When the battle's lost and won.

According to L. C. Knights,[15] both "hurlyburly" and "when the battle's lost and won" suggest the kind of metaphysical pitch-and-toss which is about to be played with good and evil, and that line 11, "Fair is foul and foul is fair," is the first statement of one of the main themes of the play, of "the reversal of values." Compare with these lines of Macbeth's witches the second of the two lines of verse which came "mysteriously" into the youthful Santiago's head:[16] "Life is lost, the battle still is won!"—of which he altered the sense by transposing two words: "Life is won, the battle still is lost!" Is this not the same kind of prophetic double-talk as: "When the battle's lost and won"?

As the witches delude Macbeth with good news and fair prophecies, so do Santiago's witches:

> . . . my thoughts ran on happiness and glory . . . An invisible fairy floated down . . . and said to me, . . . "You will be happy, Bentinho; you are going to be happy." . . . I have heard her many times, clearly and distinctly. She must be a cousin of the Scottish witches: "Thou shalt be king, Macbeth!"—"Thou shalt be happy,

Bentinho!" After all, it is the same prediction, to the selfsame tune, which is universal and eternal . . . I heard . . . José Dias's . . . "You will be happy," . . . I did not hear the rest. I heard only the voice of my inner fairy, which kept repeating to me, but now without words: "You will be happy, Bentinho!" And the voice of Capitú told me the same thing, in different words and so too that of Escobar . . . Finally, my mother . . . gave me the like prophecy, save for the editing proper to a mother: "You will be happy, my son!"[17]
Here too the language echoes *Macbeth:*

> 3. *Witch.* All hail, Macbeth! that shalt be King hereafter.
>
> .   .   .   .
>
> *Banquo.*   You shall be king.
> *Macbeth.* And Thane of Cawdor too; went it not so?
> *Banquo.* To th' self-same tune, and words.

As with Macbeth, everything and everyone conspired for Santiago's happiness, but his evil passion turned the promised happiness to self-destruction, and an atmosphere of superstition, guilt, and damnation pervades the novel. In addition to Santiago's prophetic witches, there is the strange resemblance of Capitú to Sancha's mother; of Ezekiel to Escobar. But fair is foul and foul is fair to Santiago. The fair Ezekiel foully resembles Escobar. There is the foul-fair José Dias, the foul-fair Capitú; but also the fair Bento who turns into the foul Casmurro: his miraculous birth does not prevent him from losing his soul, as Macbeth's "charmed life" does not prevent him from losing his life (and his soul). As Macbeth lost "golden opinions bought from all sorts of people," Santiago's "golden thoughts [of love] turned to ashes." There are Santiago's feelings of guilt and thoughts of damnation.[18] A supernatural gloom hovers over his determination to kill,[19] which appears as a great shadowy bird of ill omen on Friday, the day of Christ's crucifixion. There is his witches' Sabbath of brooding over the crime and buying the poison; and finally there are the ghosts that haunt him.

Hamlet too was driven to murder by supernatural influence. Santiago, like Hamlet, was under supernatural commands: Hamlet from his "saintly" father, Santiago from his "saint" mother. As Hamlet took the command of his father's ghost for a holy injunction, so Bento regarded his mother's selfish oath with superstitious awe and was bound by it, though, in reality, it was Capitú's love that was his good angel.

By thus mixing *Othello, Hamlet,* and *Macbeth,* Machado de Assis placed himself in the ranks of modern Shakespearean scholars—where, one finds a similarity of theme in *Hamlet, Macbeth,* and *Othello,*[20] another calls Hamlet and Macbeth "imaginative brothers,"[21] another links *Troilus and Cressida, Measure for Measure, Hamlet,* and *Othello,*[22] and so forth.[23]

Machado de Assis did not end his "plagiarizing" with three great tragedies. He "lifted" a couple of strokes from *Romeo and Juliet,* and a good deal from *The Winter's Tale.* When Capitú enters the story, her age is the same as Juliet's, and her Othello is only a year older. Santiago's description of her eyes recalls the lines: "My bounty is as boundless as the sea,/ My love as deep; the more I give to thee,/The more I have, for both are infinite," and "For still thy eyes, which I may call the sea,/Do ebb and flow with tears. . . ."[24]

Capitú's naturalness and lack of embarrassment over the kiss—which so amaze Bento—are Juliet's. And Santiago's rhapsody, "I stood before her as before an altar, and one side of her face was the Epistle and the other the Gospel. Her mouth the chalice, her lips the paten . . ." may be compared to the exchange between Romeo and Juliet which begins, "If I profane with my unworthiest hand/This holy shrine, the gentle fine is this:/My lips, two blushing pilgrims ready stand. . . ."

Even "the oath at the well" may derive from *Romeo and Juliet.* And there is a good chance that Santiago's "I took her at her laugh and at her word"[25] is an echo of

> *Juliet.* Take all myself.
> *Romeo.*   I take thee at thy word.
> Call me but love and I'll be new baptiz'd.

The Capitú of later scenes recalls Hermione of *The Winter's Tale.* And Santiago's jealousy bears a certain resemblance to that of Leontes. It is self-created and self-sustained like Leontes'; it is a fiery furnace for which everything serves as fuel—whether combustible or not. For example, the chance resemblance between Capitú and Gurgel's wife, which should serve as a deterrent to his suspicions, somehow only increases them. Like Leontes, he accepts his jealous imaginings as facts—to such a degree that Hermione's protest, "My life stands in the level of your dreams," and Leontes' reply, "Your actions are my dreams:/You had a bastard by Polixenes,/And I but dream'd it," might serve as a posy for the novel. Like Leontes, Santiago haled his wife before the bar of justice; and Hermione's pathetic lines at the trial, "The crown and comfort of my life, your favour,/I do give for lost; for I do feel it gone,/But know not how it went," express Capitú's inarticulate bewilderment at *her* trial. As Leontes imprisoned Hermione, Santiago banished Capitú to Switzerland and set a hireling to watch her. And then there is the resurrection. Leontes repented and Hermione came back to life. Santiago tried to resurrect the dead Capitú, but it was only a ghost that returned to haunt him.

In spite of these elements of *The Winter's Tale, Romeo and Juliet, Macbeth,* and *Hamlet* in *Dom Casmurro,* the novel remains essentially the story of an Othello, as Santiago states. A number of resemblances to *Othello* have already been noted. Let us add a few typical echoes which were passed over, recapitulate some which were barely touched upon, and examine closely what seems to be a major point of divergence.

There are echoes of conceits, phrases or turns of expression, of character and situation, and of mood—and mixtures of these various types of borrowing. Santiago's "house" (for example) has somewhat the look of Iago's "palace." "Utter my thoughts? Why, say they are vile and false;/As where's that palace whereinto foul things/Sometimes intrude not? who has a breast so pure. . . ."

The "wealthy curled darlings" of Venice whom Desdemona "shunn'd" are become the "wealthy curled darlings" ("peraltas") of Rio de Janeiro who "stared" at Capitú. "Let me see your eyes, Capitú,"[26] says Bento moved by José Dias's insinuations. "Let me see your eyes," says Othello to Desdemona. Iago called Desdemona a "supersubtle Venetian"; both he and Brabantio warned that "she did deceive her father"; Othello calls her a "subtle whore," "a closet lock and key of villainous secrets," etc. José Dias, before he gave over his role of Iago, warned Bento of Capitú's sly, gypsy's eyes the devil had given her. Santiago remarked how she deceived her father and mother; and her deceitfulness and "fine art" are the subject of his constant insinuation. Like Brabantio ("Her father loved me, oft invited me"), Padua expressed a fondness for Santiago and specifically extended the hospitality of his house to him.[27] Like Desdemona,[28] Capitú initiated the courtship—with her writing of the names on the wall and her provoking of the kiss. Desdemona's apparent confession, "Alas! he is betray'd, and I undone," is matched by Capitú's glance at Escobar's photograph —which, Santiago says, was "pure confession." Desdemona's tears for the (supposedly) dead Cassio drove Othello to the final pitch of fury, "Out, strumpet! Weep'st thou for him to my face?" Capitú's tears over

the dead Escobar spurred Santiago's relentless determination for revenge. Santiago's description of his un-
reasoning fits of jealousy,

> There is no need of an actual mortal sin, or ex-
> change of letter, simple word, nod, sigh or signal
> still more light and trifling[29] . . . a word of hers
> when dreaming[30] . . . The slightest gesture tor-
> mented me, the most casual word, the urging of a
> simple request . . . [31]

recalls Iago's way with "trifles light as air," his tale of
Cassio's talk while dreaming, and Desdemona's insistence in urging Cassio's pardon. "I did not kill her
[Justina] because I did not have handy either steel
or rope, pistol or dagger," says Santiago;[32] and Othello
says: "If there be cords or knives,/Poison or fire, or
suffocating streams,/I'll not endure it." "Why did I
marry?" asks Othello; and Santiago, "Why did I not
accomplish that wish [of my uncle's to become a
Pope]?" "I slept the next night well," remarks Othello,
"fed well, was free and merrie."[33] And Santiago, "I
eat well, and I do not sleep badly."

It might be pointed out, too, that Othello's doubt of
Desdemona's love and of his own existed before Iago
began his fiendish manipulations (II.i.192–196; III.iii.
90–92). And it was not only Iago who used the handkerchief as the principal instrument of Othello's torture;
Othello himself "lost" the handkerchief, endowed it
with magic properties, and connected it with his mother
and father. So Santiago was the first to notice the
resemblance of Escobar to Ezekiel; and he traced his
superstitious belief that sons should resemble their
fathers to his mother,[34] and loaded the belief with
mystic importance. The attitude of both Desdemona
and Capitú when faced with the "loss of the handkerchief" and the mysterious guilt attaching thereto is one
of helpless confusion and bewilderment.

The imagery of storm and shipwreck in *Othello*,
which has been discussed so frequently by Shake-

spearean scholars,[35] is used and explained by Santiago.[36]

The irony of Othello's praying and making oaths to the "marble" firmament, and calling Desdemona sinner, "devil," and "damned," while contriving his own soul's damnation, is reflected in Santiago, who, as we have seen, linked Capitú with the devil and doubted her faith while he associated himself with God and prayer, yet proceeded to the slow destruction of his love—the Christlike part of himself. It is Desdemona and Capitú who show Christian humility and forgiveness: Desdemona with her dying words, "I myself [have done this deed] . . . Commend me to my kind lord"; and Capitú with her injunctions to her son— "His mother had spoken often of me, praising me extraordinarily, as the finest man in the world, and the most worthy of being loved."[37] There is the related, or parallel, irony of "drowning the Turks" or Moors, for both Shakespeare and Machado de Assis used these terms indiscriminately. Like Othello, Santiago fought on the side of the Christians (Russians) against the Turks, but like Othello his passion turned him into a Moor—a more jealous, a more vengeful Moor.

Othello lived by the sword; his way was the violent way. Under the spell of his jealous passion he goads himself with talk of blood and cruelty; but when he comes to the act it is as swift, merciful, and passionless as he can make it. Though he has been deluded by Iago and by his own passion, he acts, as he supposes, with justice.

Like Othello, Santiago had bloody thoughts of sinking his nails into Capitú's throat, of killing her and Ezekiel by slow torture, of poisoning himself, Capitú, and Ezekiel. But there was nothing of physical violence in his background. He could not stand the sight of blood—even a mouse's; he could not poison a dog. His killings were of the neurotic variety—wishes or forgetting, that is, exclusions from his love. Yet his desire for revenge was greater than Othello's, as his jealousy was greater, more ramified, with more motivation, for in addition to the force of repression, Iago was within him, and an Iago's jealousy as well as an Othello's had to be satisfied. Iago's plans for revenge were cold and calculated: so too were Santiago's, as the Iago in his nature gained the whip hand. The chapter "The hand of Sancha" and the play on the word "contradança" even recall Iago's will to be evened with him "wife for wife." After Escobar's death it is both his Othello and Iago whose thoughts ran on revenge day and night. The result: a revenge more awful and complete than Othello's threat to "whistle her off and let her down the wind,/To prey at fortune." He spurned Capitú's love, banished her from his, from his presence, from the warmth of her friends, of her city, of her country, condemned her to lovelessness, to lonely imprisonment in the bleak and snowy Alps of Switzerland.

This death wish—this desire to "kill" Capitú by shutting her out of his love and killing his love for her—was in Santiago's heart before his jealousy—from the very beginning. In the first, adolescent quarrel, caused by Capitú's expressed doubt of his love, Bento threatens this very thing—to cut her off from his love, and himself from hers, by becoming a priest.[38] After his second attack of jealousy he makes the same threat (as has been pointed out above). For, this wish, and its execution, as in the case of the hero of *Resurreição*, springs from the feebleness of his ability to love another —from self-love. According to at least one commentator, Othello's downfall was also caused by "the inadequacy of his love" present in him from the beginning, and it was "Othello himself [who] first introduced the theme of death" into the play.[39] Once more, Machado de Assis seems merely to have anticipated modern Shakespearean interpretation.

If Othello and Santiago share a weakness of soul, it is not to be wondered at that the manifestations of Santiago's jealousy should resemble those of Othello's in minor details. Santiago points up his tendency to day-dream—the vision of the emperor, the conversation with the palm tree, "the mare," the vision of Capitú at the dying woman's house, the reliving of the kiss, the voice of the Macbethan fairy, the fantasies of shaking Capitú and of killing her, the bird of death flying on his retina, etc., etc. All these fantasies might be compared to what Iago calls Othello's "fantastical lies"—for example, of the anthropophagi, of the magical properties of the handkerchief. The emotion underlying Santiago's fantasies is, in most cases, so strong that they amount to hallucinations in which he "loses consciousness of himself and the things around him."[40] In the case of the jealous fantasies he goes into a trance or fit resembling those of Othello. Even outwardly he resembles Othello. Compare the description, "I talked to myself, persecuted myself . . . and rolled over and over with myself,"[41] with his account of the performance of *Othello*—"the Moor rolled convulsively and Iago distilled his calumny."[42] The resemblance of the inner perturbation is more marked. Compare Othello's "Chaos is come again," and "Pish! Noses, ears, and lips. —Is't possible?—Confess—handkerchief!—O devil!", with Santiago's whirling dreams "like a botched and crooked design, a confusion, a whirlwind which blinded and deafened," his "hubbub of ideas and sensations," and his "incoherencies" of handkerchiefs, sheets, shirts, and men lying dead in graveyards.[43]

There is little hint of vanity in Othello, though perhaps his readiness to believe Iago's calumny may in part be attributed to a weakness for the latter's flattery.

> *Iago.* I humbly do beseech you of your pardon
> For too much loving you.
> *Othello.*   I am bound to thee for-
>   ever.

And his "Cuckold me! . . . With mine officer!" may bear a trace of wounded vanity. But his pride in his relationship to the "great ones" of Venice bears the stamp of natural and reasonable self-esteem.

To Machado de Assis, vanity was the sine qua non of jealousy. Hence Santiago's vanity is constantly remarked.[44] The very fabric of his "handkerchief" is vanity—that his son should not resemble him, or should imitate Escobar.

The reverse of this coin—a feeling of inferiority— is not stressed so much by Santiago, but it is present. Interpreters of Shakespeare have alleged Othello's feeling of inferiority—because of his advanced age, his "race," "rough parts," lack of good looks—in excuse of his readiness to doubt Desdemona's love. The young Bento could not understand how Capitú could think him handsome and disparage her own beauty beside his, and he did not question for a second that she should prefer the other young aristocrats to him, once it was suggested to him. On his honeymoon, Santiago could not believe Capitú married him for love. Six years after marriage (he confesses) "I came to be jealous of everything and everyone. A neighbor, a partner in a waltz, any man, young or old, filled me with terror and mistrust."

This feeling of insecurity, as already pointed out, can probably be traced to his mother's betrayal of him to God, and a second time to José Dias, who caused her to repeat the betrayal by reminding her to send Bento to the seminary. As has also been mentioned, his *casmurro* insistence on Ezekiel's not being his son stems from a feeling that he is incapable of procreating a lovely boy like Ezekiel, as he is incapable of inspiring the love of a woman like Capitú.

Since his feeling of inferiority is greater than Othello's, there is less restraint and reasonable curb on his jealousy, and he shares Iago's envy and suspicion of "everyone and everything." Othello runs over Desdemona's charms,

'Tis not to make me jealous
To say my wife is fair, feeds well, loves company,
Is free of speech, sings, plays, and dances well;
Where virtue is, these are more virtuous:
Nor from my own weak merits will I draw
The smallest fear, or doubt of her revolt;
For she had eyes, and chose me.

Santiago makes the same list, but with different conclusion. Capitú loved fun and amusement, played the piano, sang, liked to dance; her beauty was admired in the street and at parties. Therefore they went to few parties; Capitú had to wear long sleeves so that men would not admire her arms; finally she did not even look out the window or come to the front door to greet her husband on his return from work, but waited behind the grilled gate of the inner apartments of the house, like an oriental—a Moorish—woman. And there is reason to believe Santiago envied Capitú her talents, as he envied Escobar his intellect and muscles, for there is a strange inconsistency, or lacuna, in the matter of her singing. In chapter lxxx he tells us Capitú's singing was the joy of his mother and her household. In chapter cv he says she gave up singing because she realized she had no voice. Does this mean that Santiago fancied himself as a singer and that Capitú gracefully withdrew from the competition?

There are other strange traces of unreason in Santiago's jealousy. His second fit, as mentioned before, was caused by pique that Escobar did not show the proper love for him by looking back from the omnibus, though the Escobar-substitute, the dandy, stared back at Capitú. That is, Santiago's despair at Escobar's rejection of him, by a strange mental process, became "Escobar loves Capitú more than me." From there it was an easy step to the inversion, "Capitú loves Escobar's substitute, the dandy, more than me," with the consequent, legitimate rage. Here we have the same situation as in *The Winter's Tale,* where Leontes' insane jealousy was roused because his childhood play-mate Polixenes refused Leontes' invitation but accepted Hermione's.

Santiago's anxious fear that Escobar loved Dona Gloria is of the same piece: he was not worried that his mother would love Escobar but only the other way round, and his relief at hearing Escobar abuse his mother is patent.[45] A related type of neurotic confusion is evinced in his identification of Sancha's and Escobar's arms.[46]

The transference of his own doubts to Dona Gloria and Justina (whom he suspected of being distant to Capitú and Ezekiel when it was *he* who was distant), and the transformation of doubt of himself into doubt of Capitú, have already been commented on.

It is only natural, perhaps, that Bento Santiago should have been jealous of everyone for whom his mother showed regard—Cosme, Justina, José Dias, Cabral, Costa, Escobar, Padua, her dead husband, God; and from his caustic references to these personages, it is apparent that he *was* jealous. It is probably normal that the child Bento should have fused his dead father with God. But there is indication of a curious double identification which seems to border on the morbid. Santiago's jealousy of Escobar did not break into the open—into full consciousness—until Escobar lay dead in his coffin, that is, until he had joined the company of God and Pedro Santiago de Albuquerque, the consorts of the "Santíssima" Gloria. But Santiago still had an Escobar-substitute on earth—Ezekiel—who was, in Santiago's eyes, a picture come to life, his old school-mate risen from the grave. The triangle continued. Santiago suspected Capitú and Ezekiel of loving each other more than they did him. He wished Ezekiel out of the way. He brooded over death by torture for both of them. Even when the grown Ezekiel returned, after Capitú's death, Santiago wished he could give him leprosy. There are two widely separated remarks which show the completeness of the identification in Santiago's mind: the first when he was taking the little boy to boarding school—"We went on foot . . . I took him by the hand, as I had taken away the other's coffin";[47] the second, upon the young man's return from Europe —"He was the self-same, the identical, the true Escobar. He was my wife's lover."[48]

Othello made provision for the murder of Cassio. As we have seen, no such revenge was possible for Santiago because of his psychic make-up. One of Machado de Assis's literary tenets was that love and jealousy are the two great masters which collaborate to produce tragedy. In developing this theme in a column of June 18, 1893,[49] he gives an illustration which seems pertinent to Santiago's case: "[Cain] could not endure it that the Lord looked only on his brother with loving eyes and, since it was not possible to kill the Lord, he killed his brother."

Santiago could not kill God, or his dead father: he obliterated his mother's memory with an anonymous tombstone. He could not kill or torture the dead Escobar: he tortured Capitú and forgot her out of existence; when she died her body remained in a nameless graveyard in Switzerland. In a neurotic sense he had fulfilled his vengeful wish for "a fire to consume her wholly and reduce her to dust, and the dust tossed to the wind, in eternal extinction."

With Capitú, the Othello in Santiago's soul died, just as Shakespeare's Othello died, though the Iago lived on. And Edward Dowden's comment on *Othello* applies equally well to *Dom Casmurro:* worse than Othello's death is Iago's way of living: "To die as Othello dies is grievous. But to live as Iago lives, devouring the dust and stinging—this is more appalling."[50]

By such psychologic alchemy did Machado de Assis transform the Moor of Venice into the Casmurro of Engenho Novo. The seed of Santiago's passion is in

Othello (and Iago), but, as Santiago's jealousy is more all inclusive, it is also more neurotic—to the point of insanity. It is as a hint of this taint, I believe, that Machado de Assis inserts a certain ironic touch in his fictitious author's book—by way of a name.

There is some insistence on Santiago's birthplace, the little hamlet of Itaguahy. Now Machado had already acquainted his readers with this place. It is the scene of one of his finest tales, "O Alienista." In this story, a native son of Itaguahy (and like Santiago born of the landed nobility), one Simon Blunderbuss, a distinguished physician with degrees from Coimbra and Padua, suffered disappointment over a little personal experiment in genetics, that is, the procreation of a "perfect son," which proved a complete fizzle, for he did not procreate anything good or bad. To compensate for his failure in this line he entered a new field, he turned alienist, and in such a big way that he eventually got the entire population of Itaguahy committed to his insane asylum. Whereupon he concluded that insanity was normal and sanity abnormal, released his inmates, and locked up himself. Whatever the interpretation placed on this story, it could not, I believe, fail to leave with Machado's readers a distinct feeling about the little city of Itaguahy and its native sons.

A trace of the same taint which attaches to Santiago's jealousy and suspicion is to be found in his revenge. Shakespeare's Othello exacted his revenge in the name of "justice." Santiago made the same claim,[51] but there are in the final chapters of the book three clear instances of his unreason and injustice.

The first is Santiago's reaction to the stage performance of *Othello,* and in particular his final conclusion:

> I heard the prayers of Desdemona, her pure and loving words, the fury of the Moor, and the death he meted out to her amid the frantic applause of the audience.

> "And she was innocent!" I kept saying to myself all down the street. "What would the audience do if she were really guilty, as guilty as Capitú? And what death would the Moor mete out to her then? A bolster would not suffice; there would be need of blood and fire, a vast, intense fire to consume her wholly, and reduce her to dust, and the dust tossed to the wind, in external extinction . . ."[52]

In this passage, there is not only the complete lack of logic which says in effect: the killing of the innocent Desdemona was just, hence in order for the "guilty Capitú's" punishment to be just it must be more terrible than Desdemona's. There is an added fillip of insanity which points to Santiago's purpose in writing his story: if he metes out a more terrible punishment to Capitú, the audience will "applaud" him still more "frantically" than they did Othello.

The second instance of injustice and unreason occurs following his accusation of Capitú.

> Death was one solution; I had just hit on another, so much the better for not being final: it opened the door to reparation, if necessary. I did not say *pardon*, but *reparation*, that is, justice.[53]

The italics are Santiago's; but, for better comprehension of his statement, the words "necessary" and "justice" should also be italicized. Again, as in the first instance, we are dealing with a very curious conception of "justice." To paraphrase his words: if, contrary to his desire, Capitú proved to be innocent, he would be just to her. He would not pardon her, that is, take her back into his heart; he would pay her damages. (What these would be, he leaves to the reader's imagination.)

Elsewhere in his writings, Machado de Assis frequently associates this type of justice with jealousy arising from "vanity" and the "pusillanimous heart."[54] The most exact parallel is to be found in an early short story, "A Mulher de Prêto," in which an innocent wife is unjustly accused of infidelity and sent by her jealous husband to live in a faraway city. Like Santiago, the husband grasps at straws of circumstantial evidence to prove his wife's guilt. When her innocence is proved to him by a friend, this is his response:

"My dear Estevam, Caesar's wife should not even be open to suspicion. I believe everything you say; but what's done is done."

"The principle is cruel, my friend."

"It is fatal."

The third indication of a weakness in Santiago's "just cause" is the unexplained lacuna already discussed above: why did Santiago fear that Capitú had gone to his mother's unless he was afraid of having the truth and its consequences forced upon him?

These three instances, it seems to me, demonstrate that it was not justice Santiago was after, but only the consummation of his death wish—the desire to be done with loving Capitú. Like Felix of *Resurreição* his heart was dead, he *could not* requite her great love. According to John Money,[55] Othello suffered from a similar "impotence," as he calls it. Money makes the further point that Othello's setting himself up as minister of divine justice, as the just instrument of Fate or Destiny is self delusion, and that the divinity to which Othello and Iago kneel "is the fixity of their own wills"—the will to destroy arising from their "impotence" to create. In Othello's case is included "the will to see things as they are not."

The words of the jealous husband of "A Mulher de Prêto," "It is fatal" might almost be an echo of Othello's "So sweet was ne'er so fatal," (as his previous "What's done is done" is certainly a quote from *Macbeth*). Yet earlier in the story this man uses John Money's line: "'Destiny is will,' replied Menezes, 'Each man makes his own destiny.'"

Santiago, too, attributed the cause of his tragedy to destiny—particularly in the chapters "A dramatic reform" and "The stage manager," and in his closing words to his jury of readers, "One thing remains, . . . to wit, that my first love and my greatest friend . . . were destined to . . . deceive me."

We have already seen that in *Dom Casmurro*, as in Machado's other writings, destiny and nature are the same: a man's destiny *is* his nature. With this final statement, Santiago would have us believe it was Capitú's and Escobar's deceitful natures which caused the downfall of the loving Bento. Indeed, in the sentence preceding it, he uttered the dictum that the later deceitful Capitú was in the earlier like the fruit within its rind, though we discovered his words were applicable to himself rather than to Capitú (that it was his Casmurro nature which broke through the rind of Bento Santiago). The same, according to Money, is true of Othello, who calls Desdemona's infidelity "the cause." "But there is ambiguity, too, in Othello's appeal to his own soul to justify 'the cause.' For there is a sense in which his soul *is* 'the cause.' "[56]

Thus, the ending of *Dom Casmurro* not only echoes *Othello*, as I suggested in the beginning of this chapter, it reproduces the ending of Othello. T. S. Eliot has the following to say on Othello's speech of self-justification ("Soft you; . . ."):

> What Othello seems to me to be doing in making this speech is *cheering himself up*. He is endeavouring to escape reality, he has ceased to think about Desdemona, and is thinking about himself . . . Othello succeeds in turning himself into a pathetic figure, by adopting an *aesthetic* rather than a moral attitude, dramatising himself against his environment. He takes in the spectator, but the human motive is primarily to take in himself. I do not believe that any writer has ever exposed this *bovaryisme*, the human will to see things as they are not, more clearly than Shakespeare.[57]

John Money quotes this passage, and adds in conclusion: "To see Othello as he wishes himself to be seen is to distort the tragedy."

Bento Santiago, I submit, also has the will to see things as they are not. Like Othello he tries to delude "the spectator"—his readers—for if they applaud him more frantically than they did Othello, they exonerate him; his self-delusion will be complete, he will be cleared of guilt in his own eyes, his conscience will be free.[58] But if we the readers see him "as he wishes himself to be seen," we "distort the tragedy."

Once again modern Shakespearean criticism is of a piece with Machado de Assis's interpretation.

11

An Interesting Case of Anonymity

WITH THE FOREGOING CHAPTERS of this study I have
tried to suggest an answer to the question posed at
the beginning of it: was Capitú guilty of infidelity?
But, as stated then, the complete answer hinges upon
the answer to a subsidiary question: why did Machado
de Assis leave the decision to the reader? If Santiago,
like Othello, was self-deluded, why did Machado de
Assis not pass judgment upon him—as he did so conclusively on Felix of *Resurreição?* Why did he allow
his hero to "dramatize himself" for the reader, and
leave the reader to pass judgment on him? The answer
to the second question, as to the first, is, I believe, to
be sought in Machado's artistic method.

Practically all the characters in *Dom Casmurro* are
named—and, as I attempted to show, carefully named.
Even persons to whom there is only a passing reference
—as Bento's schoolmates Borges, the Albuquerques,
and Bastos, Capitú's friend Paula, and slaves in the
Santiago household—are given names. But there is one
person of some prominence whose name Santiago deliberately withholds, and makes such a to-do about not
giving his name that one's curiosity is aroused. I refer
to the anonymous author of the *Panegyric of Saint
Monica.* Why this "lacuna"? And why is the nameless
man and his panegyric introduced into the story at all?

Is this episode a digression? Why would Machado de Assis, one of the most economical of writers, permit a digression in this, his masterpiece, which is also a masterpiece of economy? Because, it would seem, he could not help himself, in view of the method he had adopted for the construction of this novel.

In the novel which followed *Dom Casmurro, Esaú e Jacob,* the narrator (who, as has been remarked before, bore more resemblance to Machado de Assis than ever Bento Santiago did) explains his method of writing. He says that the line of Dante, "Dico che quando l'anima mal nata," which one of the characters wrote in his diary, could serve as posy to the book because it is not only a means of rounding out the characters and their ideas but is also "a pair of spectacles with which the reader may penetrate whatever seems not quite clear or wholly obscure." And he goes on:

> Furthermore, there is an advantage in having the characters of my story collaborate in it, aiding the author in accordance with a law of solidarity, a kind of exchange of services between the chess-player and his men.

> If you accept the comparison, you will recognize the King and the Queen, the Bishop and the Knight, and that the Knight cannot become a Castle, nor the Castle a Pawn. There is of course the difference of color, white and black, but this does not affect the power of each piece to move, and finally one side or the other wins the game, and so goes the world. Perhaps it would have been a good idea to insert, from time to time, (as in chess books) the favorable positions or the difficult ones. With no chessboard, that procedure is a great aid for following the moves, but then it may be that you have enough vision to reproduce the various situations from memory. Yes, I think so. To heck with diagrams! Everything will go along as if you were actually witnessing a game between

two players or, to be more precise, between God and the devil.[1]

From our examination of the "opera" and the "married couple" in *Dom Casmurro* we know that "the game between God and the devil" means the good and the evil in the characters moving them this way and that.[2] In other words, the characters are completely autonomous: the good and evil in their natures make the action; the characters "write" the story.

This literary device, explained so carefully in *Esaú e Jacob*, Machado de Assis had already put into practice in *Dom Casmurro*. But *Dom Casmurro* is a story within a story: the fictitious Santiago is the author of the narrative proper, and there is no reason to believe he used Machado's artistic device. On the contrary, there is reason to believe he colored his narrative, consciously and unconsciously, for he had a personal motive in writing it—to clear himself before the bar of public opinion and his own conscience. The fact remains, however, that it was Machado de Assis who created the several characters of the novel (including Santiago); and their actions spring from the natures *he* gave them. If there are inconsistencies and gaps ("lacunae") in Santiago's reporting, nevertheless the characters are there as Machado de Assis created them, and by ferreting out the flaws in Santiago's account and reading between his lines we should be able to arrive at the truth.

Machado de Assis not only created the characters, he also named them. Apparently Santiago faithfully reported their names—if he knew or remembered them or considered them worthy of his notice—with the exception of the author of the panegyric. This "lacuna," like Santiago's other "lacunae," I take it, is "a pair of spectacles" which the real author places on our noses for clearer vision. And it is, like the writing of the line of Dante, a spontaneous act on the part of a created character—with whom Machado de Assis, having committed himself to a policy of divine aloofness, could not interfere.

With the insulting omission of the name, and the subsequent sarcastic portrayal of its bearer and his pitiful opus, Santiago turns on his maker: the anonymous author, I believe, is none other than Machado de Assis himself. At first glance the idea may seem far-fetched, not to say preposterous. But let us consider three ingredients of the episode: Santiago's pompous condescension, the superficial resemblances between Machado and the panegyrist, and the subject of the panegyric—Saint Monica.

That Santiago should turn his sarcastic wit upon the author of his being is not to be wondered at, but, rather, to be expected. He does the same for all his friends and relations, including his mother, God, and, at times, himself. He drags in the Emperor Pedro II and holds *him* up to ridicule—his love of pomp and preoccupation with philanthropies, that is, in his role of "Pedro Bananas."[3] Why should he stick at belaboring Machado de Assis? And there is a matter of professional jealousy. In his very first chapter Santiago makes a remark that causes one to wonder: "There are books which owe no more [than the title] to their authors; some, not so much." Is this a slurring glance at the man whose name appears on his title page? However that may be, Santiago makes no bones of his literary pretensions. In chapter ii, he lists the subjects on which he feels qualified to write—jurisprudence, philosophy, politics—and intimates that he could compose a better history of Rio de Janeiro than the classic *Memoirs* of Padre Luiz Gonçalves dos Santos. Later he points to his accomplishments in the literary line: two verses of a sonnet, "other things in prose," and "now this narrative."[4] "This narrative," as the reader well knows, contains a certain element of fiction—which brings him into direct competition with Machado de Assis. Santiago reduces it to nothing by burying his master and his maker in anonymity, just as he buried his mother in anonymity with the epitaph "Saint." Machado's epitaph is less flattering. He is represented (through his anonymous counterpart) as a ridiculous little clerk in a government office who fancies himself as a writer because he once wrote a worthless little book—a panegyric of St. Monica, dedicated to St. Augustine— an old-fashioned piece filled with dull quotations from the classics. He has gone through life dispensing copies of it. There's only one thing to be said for him: he's an efficient public servant.

There is little apparent resemblance between Santiago's portrait and the real Machado de Assis. But before examining it in detail, let us take a look at the one fictional character which Machado de Assis acknowledged as a self-portrait—Aguiar of *Memorial de Ayres*[5] —for he too bears little resemblance to Machado in minor details of biography. Aguiar married Carmo (Carolina) when he was a bookkeeper, and rose to be a banker. His wife, before marriage, lived with her mother (who came from Nova Friburgo) and father (who was a Swiss watchmaker from the same city). The marriage was "favored by everyone." Soon after the marriage Aguiar lost his job, Carmo weathered the hard times with cheerfulness, bolstered up her husband, made furnishings for their house with her own hands. Aguiar had a poetic flair which evinced itself in his conversation, though he had never written anything. "If he had written," comments Ayres, "[Carmo] would have found him better than anyone, because she truly loved him, as much or more than on the first day." Aguiar liked to read literature but had little time for it; his wife read, and wrote résumés and comments in a little notebook for her busy husband.[6]

Now Machado de Assis had never been a bookkeeper of course, and he was never a banker. His wife Carolina was Portuguese; her father *had* been in the jewelry business but in Portugal, not Brazil. When Machado met her, her mother and father were dead, she had come to Rio de Janeiro to be with her brother, the poet Faustino Xavier de Novaes; soon after, another brother and a sister joined them. There is some doubt as to whether both brothers at least "favored the marriage."[7] The hard times are real.[8] Carmo's devotion in all its details may be presumed to be that of Carolina. According to Lúcia Miguel Pereira, Carolina did keep such a notebook as described by Ayres, for the use of Machado in his writing.[9] The companionship of the old couple in their secluded and rather lonely life is surely Carolina and Machado. And there must have been something in Aguiar's simple and unaffected courting of friendship, in his quiet admiration for his lively wife, his mild air of enthusiasm and hopefulness, which Machado's friends recognized as his.[10] But there is really very little here to identify Aguiar to Machado de Assis's reading public.

To return to Santiago's panegyrist. He, like Machado, was a public servant, and Santiago admits that he was an efficient public servant. "In 1882" he was working as "head of a division of the Navy Department." In 1882 Machado de Assis was head of a division of the Agriculture Department.[11] And Machado de Assis prided himself on being an honest and efficient public servant.[12] The panegyrist was an ex-seminarist, but it is believed Machado de Assis received some of his early education from a priest and that he worked around a church.[13] The same modest friendliness and contentment with simple blessings displayed by Aguiar are found in the panegyrist—who was content with his one modest literary effort, content with Santiago's half-hearted display of interest in it. Like Machado, he at least considered himself a literary man. Yes, but the author of one wretched little obscure book! and Machado de Assis's writings, even in 1882, filled thousands of pages; he was well known and had attained some popularity! The subject of the panegyric converts this apparent point of difference into the conclusive bit of evidence for identifying the panegyrist.

In 1850 there was established in Paris an association of Christian mothers under the patronage of St. Monica: its object mutual prayer for wayward sons and husbands. Because, of course, it was through Monica's love and saintly efforts that her cruel and wayward husband was converted to Christianity, and her wayward, philandering son Augustine was brought back into the fold. St. Augustine is often quoted and referred to by Machado de Assis. Indeed, he frequently compares himself to St. Augustine. Quincas Borba, who is certainly intended to represent Brazil, or an aspect of it, says, in his madness, "I am St. Augustine."[14] The protagonist-narrator of the novelette *Casa Velha* likens himself to St. Augustine: " 'Amor non improbatur [Love is not condemned],' wrote my great Saint Augustine. The main thing for him, as for me, is that God's creatures be loved and love in God."[15] The father of the twins in *Esaú e Jacob* is named for St. Augustine, as his sister-in-law has the same name as the saint's sister. This father (along with his wife and sister-in-law) devotes himself to trying to make his twin sons love each other.

That Machado de Assis should identify Brazilian men (and himself as one of them) with Augustine, and Brazilian womanhood with St. Monica, is superficially appropriate for two reasons. Brazilian (and Portuguese) men of the nineteenth century were notoriously wayward sons and faithless husbands. Monica and Augustine were Africans, by some thought to have been of Negro origin: there is a large African element in the Brazilian population, and Machado himself had Negro blood.

The men Machado de Assis portrays in his fiction are, for the most part, the sons of women, not men. In *Dom Casmurro* not only is Santiago the son of his mother but even Dona Gloria is the daughter of her mother, and *her* mother the daughter of a mother.[16] It has been remarked that Machado de Assis's women are frequently better portrayed and stronger characters than his men.[17]

In other words, Machado de Assis's writings, taken as a whole, form a "panegyric of St. Monica," of the Brazilian woman, and all women. But St. Monica is also a made to order symbol for love, and St. Augustine a symbol of the human soul as a battle ground for love and self-love. Thus, the panegyric of St. Monica becomes a description, in a broader sense, of Machado's artistic purpose—to portray the good, Christian mother, that is, the goodness in human nature, working upon her wayward son, who is sometimes saved, sometimes lost. Hence Machado de Assis submits without protest to Santiago's portrait, which in his own words might run somewhat as follows: My writing is a panegyric of St. Monica (love), which I dedicate to St. Augustine (my fellow Brazilians, and all mankind). Santiago calls it old-fashioned: well, it is not of the modern, naturalistic school; but based on the old classic writers. I go through life dispensing copies (my various works, which all have the same theme). My panegyric seems important to me, but perhaps it is of no importance. At any rate, I am an honest and efficient public servant.

And in this very novel *Dom Casmurro,* Machado de Assis is "dispensing his panegyric," is thrusting it upon the fictional author Santiago, just as the anonymous panegyrist of the story forced a copy on him. Santiago partially admits the analogy. He says his own panegyric was the sonnet,[18] but the "sonnet" signifies his "life," and *Dom Casmurro* is the account of his life. He also tells us he improved upon the *Panegyric of Saint Monica:* "I put into it not only what it lacked of the saint, but also things which had nothing to do with her."[19] Later he implies that this only "makes the saint more saintly."[20] At the same time he identifies the saint with his mother. As usual his interpretation is confused: Dona Gloria *is* one aspect of Machado de Assis's "saint"; but the most perfect embodiment of Saint Monica is Capitú. And Capitú shines through Santiago's narrative in spite of him, for she is thrust upon him by the master panegyrist, Machado de Assis.

The episode of the panegyric, then, is "a pair of spectacles" which Machado de Assis sets on the reader's nose, so that he may see that Santiago is not the real author of the book—and may see who is. Since its narration is a spontaneous act on Santiago's part, the episode also "rounds out his character" by affording a prime example of his powers at coloring fact. In *Esaú e Jacob* the reader is told that he, as well as the characters, should collaborate with the author[21]—that the highest enjoyment of a literary work, the greatest instruction from it, is to be obtained only if the reader exerts all his powers of observation, reason, imagination and understanding, and becomes an interpreter. Thus Machado de Assis leaves the reader of *Dom Casmurro* to pass judgment on the innocence of Capitú, on the justice of Santiago's revenge—and he leaves Santiago free to tell his story as he will.

But Machado de Assis never evinced much faith in jury trials.[22] In Santiago's case, he no doubt anticipated that the trial, at best, would result in a hung jury. In his little discursus on Cain and Abel (part of which was quoted above), he wrote:

> The human plant requires blood, as the other plants dew. We all deplore the death of Abel, from a habit of schooling and upbringing; but the truth is that Cain set a powerful example for future generations. Having presented the Lord with the first fruits of his tilling, as Abel had presented the firstlings of his flock, he could not endure it that the Lord looked only on his brother with loving eyes; and, since it was not possible to

kill the Lord, he killed his brother. Thus was born iniquity, which is the *grano salis* of this world. Santiago's remark apropos of the frantic applause of the audience for the killing of the innocent Desdemona (What would the audience do if the Moor meted out a worse punishment to a Desdemona as guilty as Capitú?) echoes Machado's "grano salis," and looks forward to the decision of the jury. The human plant requires blood! As G. W. Knight says of Desdemona, we all "slay Desdemona half a dozen times most days of our life."[23] We all have a trace of *casmurro* in our make-up—a self-love which makes us prone to suspect, envy, and hate what is better than ourselves, to sympathize with what is worse, or no better.

The panegyric episode discloses Machado's fear that the jury will be taken in by Santiago and let him go scot-free. But if we do our part as readers, the part Machado de Assis assigned us, we will see that Santiago was not the author of the book. And then we will find a certain irony in Santiago's statement that he put things into the panegyric which had nothing to do with the saint but which made her more saintly; for this is only another way of saying "God writes straight with crooked lines"—God in this case, of course, being Machado de Assis. We will see that the love symbolized by Capitú does not suffer defeat: it triumphs, just as the good symbolized by Cordelia triumphed against evil, and *Dom Casmurro* is no more a work of pessimism than is *King Lear*.[24] In praising a certain good man, Machado de Assis once wrote:

> The great man awes us, the glory of the famous dazzles, we are carried away by the bold deeds of brave men. Goodness does not produce any of these effects. And yet there is a grandeur, there is a glory and a valor in being simply good, without display, without interest, without calculation; and above all without regret.[25]

159

To which Santiago would retort, "Yes, virtue is its own reward." Because the aim of the fictional author of *Dom Casmurro* and that of the real author are diametrically opposed. Machado would persuade us of the beauty of love. Santiago converts us to self-love.

12

"Saint Monica" and the
"Plagiarist"

THE BRAZILIAN CRITIC José Veríssimo divided Machado de Assis's novels into two periods; and practically all writers on Machado de Assis since have accepted this division: the first four comprising what is sometimes called his "romantic" period, the later ones his "second" or "mature" style.[1] Machado smiled at this division, and protested that all his novels, along with his other books, were each a milestone in his life of the spirit.[2] From one point of view, I believe, his amused bewilderment is justified; from another, the division made by his critics is surely proper.

Life, he said, was a struggle between God and the devil, between the good and evil in men's souls. It is generally agreed that his novels are a probing into the soul. But, as I have tried to show, good and evil to Machado were love and self-love. Thus we find the theme of love versus self-love running through all nine novels—through all his fiction, indeed, and perhaps through his writing as a whole.

He enunciated this theme in his first published book, an essay entitled *A Queda que as Mulheres Têm para os Tolos*[3] ("the weakness women have for *tolos*"). Though this is a humorous essay, so that it is difficult to decide where the author stands in the matter, he seems to display a certain personal bias in favor of the "homens de espírito" ("men of intelligence, taste, and sensibility") as opposed to the "tolos" ("brash fellows with little intellect, no imagination, and none of the finer feelings"). Eleven years later, in his first novel, *Resurreição,* his position is almost exactly reversed, with the "homem de espírito" exhibit A for self-love. In succeeding works of fiction he experimented with various ingredients and obtained various alloys of love and self-love. Thus one finds self-love manifesting itself as ambition, jealousy, insatiability, vanity, pride, fear, and so on. There are curious mixtures of the various manifestations; there are admixtures of love to self-love, as lust, and the egoism which attracts others to itself (as a whale attracts barnacles) and loves them as a part of its own skin. Comedy enters the struggle with its grotesque paradoxes, compromises, mock battles, and inglorious victories. Still, the posy to the first novel, could serve as posy to them all. "Our doubts are traitors,/And make us lose the good we oft might win,/ By fearing to attempt." It is only necessary to read for "doubts," "self-love" and for "good," "love"—as he carefully explained in that novel.

His last novel, *Memorial de Ayres,* is the answer, the happy ending, as it were, to the first: it *is Resurrection.* The diplomat Ayres is a Felix whose "dead heart" was "resurrected" permanently. Ayres, by virtue of his profession, had passed his life in a war of wits and hypocrisy, suspecting everyone, loving no one (or only very few very little). He married for professional reasons, and like Santiago, buried his wife in the old country without any pangs to speak of, and forgot her.[4] As he remarked upon his widowhood, he was "a bachelor by nature";[5] he was also a philanderer.[6] Then he retired and came home to Brazil—like an Odysseus (it is he who suggests the comparison)[7] who had reached Ithaca, naked, cold, and shaken by wars (diplomacy)[8] and encounters with Neptune, and with only a few

tepid memories of pleasant sojourns in nymphs' grot-
toes.[9] There, in the warmth of his native Rio de
Janeiro,[10] basking in the loving example of Rita
(sisterly love), Fidelia (wifely love), and Carmo
(mother-love), his love was reborn.[11]

In the beginning of his *Memorial,* before this regen-
eration is complete, Ayres offers to make a wager with
Rita that the devoted widow Fidelia will break her
vow and remarry: he likens it to the wager between
God and Mephistopheles over the soul of Faust. At the
end of the book, Fidelia does remarry, but Ayres writes
in his diary that he believes her love for the second
husband is a part and continuation of her love for the
first, and he adds:

> When I was an active member of the diplomatic
> corps I did not believe so many things could be all
> stuck up together; I was suspicious and distrust-
> ful. But if I retired, it was for the very purpose of
> believing in the sincerity of others. Let the fellows
> who are still active do the distrusting![12]

There are hints of this coming "resurrection" even
in *Esaú e Jacob* (the novel to which *Memorial de Ayres*
forms a sequel): " 'Love is a duel, not to the death, but
to the life,' concluded Ayres with a faint smile."[13] That
is, if overcome by love, one does not die but comes
to life, for love has creative powers. And he seems to
look forward to his own heart's progress toward complete resurrection with another comment, on one of
the characters, who had rounded the Cape of Storms
(lust and self-love) and was peacefully pursuing the
route to India.[14]

These two remarks by the old diplomat sum up the
theme of Machado's writing, and of his "life." Machado
de Assis believed in his own spiritual progress. Because
it was consistent and rapid he at times, no doubt, became gloomy or impatient with the slow journey of
humankind.[15] He believed human progress possible,
but not inevitable, not to be achieved without struggle.

He refused to admit that his century had gained the heights; he refused to recognize as evidence of advance, empty victories and insecure positions, for he thought complacency with dubious gains impeded progress.[16] He was not uninterested in social and economic reforms through law and political agitation, as has sometimes been claimed:[17] he grasped at everything that might help man forward. Not only was he engaged in active politics and political writing in his early years, some of his short stories portray cruel conditions of poverty and other forms of slavery.[18] But, as a part of his progress, he became increasingly convinced that such efforts, at best, could bring about only temporary and spotty amelioration. For permanent cure it was necessary to go beneath the surface, to uncover the protean forms of self-love which nourished the visible poverty, ignorance, and corruption he saw about him. And his belief grew that the writer had the most to contribute,[19] for it is the poetic, the creative, writer who explores and lays bare the human soul with its locked struggle between love and self-love.

He was concerned with humanity, but in particular with that of his own country.[20] He was proud of Brazil's progress and its heritage. He believed in its future, that it could best serve civilization by studying itself and using its own heritage. As a writer, he considered the Portuguese language a beautiful and powerful tool, to be improved and used;[21] for he saw it being debased through ignorance, neglect, scorn, and despair—and even abandoned by some of his contemporaries in favor of a foreign language.[22] He has been called the most Brazilian of all his country's writers,[23] as no doubt he is; yet there is in his fictional works almost nothing of what generally passes for "local color." He admired such writers as Alencar, who extolled the physical beauty of his country, and he himself was far from insensible to that beauty. But he considered the soul

of the Carioca far more beautiful than the Bay of
Guanabara, the attainments of the Luso-Brazilian far
more admirable than the exploits of the Tupí. He
considered mooning about the past and the natural
beauty of Brazil a hindrance to the growth of the
Brazilian soul, which, he felt, was essentially European
and Portuguese.[24]

Though he recognized the Brazilian soul as individual and distinct, he saw it as an integral part of the
soul of humanity, so that the poetic writer should not
limit himself to time or place. It is in those terms that
he defined the role of poet, dramatist, fabulist, and
novelist. For example:

> We celebrate . . . the writer [Almeida Garrett],
> one of the greatest of our language, one of the first
> of the century, and the one who joins in his books
> the soul of the nation with the life of human-
> ity.[25]

> I ask whether *Hamlet, Othello, Julius Caesar,
> Romeo and Juliet* have anything in common with
> English history, or British territory, and if, never-
> theless, Shakespeare is not, besides being a uni-
> versal genius, an essentially English poet.[26]

> Malta's muse is also a traveler and a cosmopolite.
> Wherever he finds material ready to hand he
> does not reject it but gathers it up, adorns it, com-
> bines it with other gatherings, and offers it to his
> country.[27]

The best way of comprehending the universal soul of
mankind, said Machado, was through study of great
writers the world over; the best way of portraying it
was by "plagiarizing" them.

> The French Revolution and *Othello* have been
> written: still there is nothing to prevent one from
> lifting this or that scene and using it in other

dramas: thus are committed, literarily speaking, acts of plagiarism.[28]

Again, in commenting on Musset's *Les Nuits:*

"Mon verre n'est pas grand, mais je bois dans mon verre."

A little cup, but of fine gold, filled with pure wine, wine from all the vintages, Gallic, Spanish, Italian, and Greek, with which he inebriated himself and his century and is about to make drunk the century that is dawning.[29]

It is the same with Machado's cup, which holds not only Brazilian wine but wines from Albion, Spain, France, Italy, and Greece. The most patent single example of his practice in this kind of mixing may be seen in the names used in *Dom Casmurro,* which we discussed at such length. Those real names handed down from Portuguese forebears have a Luso-Brazilian poetry of their own, but, in addition, they have been infused with a wealth of imagery and significance drawn from universal poesy.

This fusion of the Brazilian soul with the soul of humanity had been Machado de Assis's practice all along—hence his mild surprise at Veríssimo's division of his novels into two classes or styles. But with his fifth novel he expanded this artistic practice in a certain definite way—which makes his last five novels at once less Brazilian than the first four, and more so. In the last five novels he transplanted to Brazilian soil whole classics, or classic genres, taken from literatures other than the Luso-Brazilian. Thus, he used as the basis for *Memórias Póstumas de Braz Cubas* three foreign novels of one genre (one Spanish, one French, one English), for *Quincas Borba,* a single Spanish classic, for *Esaú e Jacob,* Greek tragedy, for *Memorial de Ayres,* Greek epic. In *Dom Casmurro* he "offered his country" a Brazilian *Othello.* And because Shakespeare spoke louder and clearer to him than all other men,[30] because Shakespeare was "universal poetry,"[31] was "humanity real and true,"[32] because Shakespeare *was* "the human soul,"[33] *Dom Casmurro* is Machado's masterpiece and the brightest cluster in the great galaxy of Brazilian literature.

Appendix:
Biography of Machado de Assis

ALTHOUGH three of Machado de Assis's novels have now been translated into English, his name is still absent from our encyclopedias and biographical dictionaries. He was born in Rio de Janeiro on June 21, 1839, and christened, the following November, Joaquim Maria Machado de Assis. His father, Francisco José de Assis, was a native of Rio de Janeiro, the son of "free" mulattoes. His mother, Maria Leopoldina Machado de Assis, was a Portuguese woman from the Azores. These facts are learned from baptismal and marriage certificates. The only other precise information extant on his parents is their street address for 1845, which is listed in the *Laemmert Almanach,* to which his father was a subscriber.

Machado had a younger sister who died, as did his mother, when he was a child. Rumor has it the father remarried. He too died early—while Machado was still in grammar school. How the boy lived and what became of the stepmother—if indeed he had a stepmother—are matters of speculation among his biographers. (Machado in later years told his friend José Veríssimo that he had been poor in his youth.) One of his early poems is dedicated to a cousin but nothing else has been learned about him. There is no mention of any other relatives.

Nothing further is heard of Machado de Assis until his fifteenth year, when a poem appeared over his signature in a ladies' fashion magazine. Henceforth his professional activities, at least, are easy to trace. At seventeen he was a typesetter, at nineteen, a proof-reader, at twenty-one, a reporter. For the rest of his sixty-nine years, we can follow him in and out of one newspaper, magazine, and publishing establishment after another. His writings poured forth in a steady stream: poems, criticism, columns of witty and pene-trating commentary on passing events, translations from French and English, plays, short stories, and novels. From 1873 his meager income as a writer was augmented by a position with the Ministry of Agri-culture, where he continued to serve until his last ill-ness in 1908. Many honors in recognition of his writing were bestowed on him, the first by the emperor in 1867. And finally, when the Brazilian Academy of Letters was founded in 1897, he was elected its first president and perpetually reëlected.

Such was Machado de Assis, the writer of reputation, plodding journalist, and exemplary civil servant—never missing a day at the office—never venturing more than a few miles beyond the city limits of his native Rio de Janeiro.

When we turn to his fiction—the nine novels and over two hundred shorter pieces of his collected works —we find a Machado who has traveled far, through past ages, into the depths of men's souls. As he tells his tales, we see the steady, consistent emergence of an intellect, of a conception of the writing art and the role of the artist in human progress. His critical essays and journal-istic columns serve as footnotes and marginalia to the fictional works.

From the columns and from his correspondence we also get our only intimate glimpses of Machado de Assis in his daily life—of his habits, of his likes, and of his dislikes; his love of his native city, dismay over its lack of health ordinances; his witty impatience with crooked politics, patent medicines, Sarah Bernhardt, the high cost of dying, after-dinner speakers, and other glorious products of civilization; his eagerness to hold out a helping hand to other Brazilian writers, young and old; his pride in the Portuguese language; passionate devotion to Shakespeare; discussions of literature over a cup of tea; his friendships; his loneliness after his wife died.

He was married thirty-five years to the same woman, Carolina Novaes (sister of the Portuguese poet Faustino Xavier de Novaes); and they left behind them in our dull world, a legend of conjugal devotion that bedims the Brownings'.

In physical appearance Machado de Assis was short, straight, and slight; his face and head, as revealed by the death mask, were strong and, in the larger sense of the word, beautiful. He apparently suffered from epilepsy all his life but more especially when he was young and during his last four years—after the death of Carolina. (Some notes on the attacks, which he wrote for his physician during the latter period, are extant.)

He died in his native city on September 29, 1908. The Chamber of Deputies, in a special session, voted a state funeral with civil and military honors. This was the first time in the history of Brazil (as Graça Aranha tells us) that a simple man of letters was buried like a hero. All over Brazil long speeches (of the type Machado abhorred) were delivered about him. In France a memorial session was held at the Sorbonne, with Anatole France presiding.

The enshrining of Machado de Assis has continued through the years. During the centennial year, 1939, seventeen books and upwards of five hundred articles by three hundred and fifty writers were published about him in Brazil. Books and articles continue to pour forth, with new writers constantly joining the ranks.

Notes

UNLESS otherwise indicated, writings of Machado de Assis mentioned in the text and in the notes of this study may be found in the following three collections.

(1) *Obras Completas de Machado de Assis,* published by W. M. Jackson Inc., Rio de Janeiro (from 1937), thirty-one volumes, which are all in print:

Novels

RESURREIÇÃO
A MÃO E A LUVA
HELENA
YAYÁ GARCIA
MEMORIAS POSTHU-
   MAS DE BRAZ
   CUBAS
QUINCAS BORBA
DOM CASMURRO
ESAÚ E JACOB
MEMORIAL DE AYRES

Poetry

POESIAS COMPLETAS

Drama

THEATRO

Correspondence

CORRESPONDENCIA

Short stories

CONTOS FLUMINENSES, I, II
HISTORIAS DA MEIA NOITE
HISTORIAS ROMANTICAS
PAPEIS AVULSOS
HISTORIAS SEM DATA
VARIAS HISTORIAS
PAGINAS RECOLHIDAS
   (also contains speeches)
RELIQUIAS DE CASA VELHA,
   I, II (Vol. I also contains sonnet
   "A Carolina")

Criticism and commentary

CRITICA LITTERARIA
CRITICA THEATRAL
CHRONICAS, I, II, III, IV
A SEMANA, I, II, III

Since the pagination of these volumes varies from printing to printing, this study contains no reference to them by page, but only by chapter, column dateline, and so on.

(2) Eight volumes of short stories and columns from periodicals, edited by R. Magalhães Junior, and published by Editora Civilização S/A, Rio de Janeiro, 1956–1958:

CONTOS AVULSOS
CONTOS E CRÔNICAS

CONTOS ESPARSOS
CONTOS ESQUECIDOS
CONTOS RECOLHIDOS
CONTOS SEM DATA
CRÔNICAS DE LÉLIO
DIÁLOGOS E REFLEXÕES DE UM RELOJOEIRO
(3) POESIA E PROSA, edited by J. Galante de Sousa, published by Editora Civilização Brasileira S/A, Rio de Janeiro, 1957.

* * *

Three of the novels have been published in English, by the Noonday Press, New York: *Memórias Póstumas de Braz Cubas*, under the title *Epitaph of a Small Winner*, translated by William L. Grossman (1952); *Dom Casmurro*, translated by Helen Caldwell (1953); *Quincas Borba*, under the title *Philosopher or Dog?*, translated by Clothilde Wilson (1954).

An English translation of three of the short stories, "O Enfermeiro," "Viver," and "A Cartomante," will be found in Isaac Goldberg, *Brazilian Tales* (Boston, The Four Seas Co., 1921), under the titles "The Attendant's Confession," "Life," and "The Fortune-Teller."

PREFACE

[1] E.g., Álvaro Lins, *Jornal de Crítica: Primeira Série* (Rio, Olympio, 1941), p. 171; Alceu Amoroso Lima, *Três Ensaios Sôbre Machado de Assis* (Belo Horizonte, Paulo Bluhm, 1941), pp. 13, 70; Barreto Filho, *Introdução a Machado de Assis* (Rio, A.G.I.R., 1947), pp. 7, 34; Lúcia Miguel Pereira, *Machado de Assis: Estudo Crítico e Biográfico* (5th ed.; Rio, Olympio, 1955), p. 277; Bezerra de Freitas, *Forma e Expressão no Romance Brasileiro* (Rio, Pongetti, 1947), p. 140.

[2] Even Lúcia Miguel Pereira, in her excellent *Machado de Assis: Estudo Crítico e Biográfico*, attempts to trace in Machado's characters the influence of his epilepsy and of his acute consciousness of his Negro blood and humble origin. Cf. Óthon Costa, "Machado de Assis Epiléptico," in his *Conceitos e Afirmações* (Rio, Pongetti [1939]), pp. 73–86; Vianna Moog, *Heróis da Decadência* (Porto Alegre, Globo, 1939), pp. 208–209; Peregrino Junior, *Doença e Constituição de Machado de Assis* (Rio, Olympio, 1938); Hermínio de Brito Conde, *A Tragédia Ocular de Machado de Assis* (Rio, 1942); Sylvio Romero, *Machado de Assis* (2d ed.; Rio, Olympio, 1936), pp. 54–55 (the effect of Machado's stuttering on his style).

[3] For example, he did not wish any of his correspondence published (letter of April 21, 1908, to José Veríssimo, and Veríssimo's replies of April 23 and 24 [CORRESPONDENCIA]), and gave a specific

order that the letters exchanged between him and his wife, along
with other keepsakes, should be burned upon his death (Lúcia Miguel
Pereira, *Machado de Assis*, p. 112). Cf. *ibid.*, p. 22; Augusto Meyer,
"Introdução," *Exposição Machado de Assis: Centenário do Nascimento
de Machado de Assis 1839–1939*, ed. Instituto Nacional do Livro
(Rio, 1939), p. 13.

⁴ As in his 1907 foreword to *A Mão e a Luva*, or in his foreword to
Relíquias de Casa Velha (RELIQUIAS DE CASA VELHA, I).

⁵ This oft repeated advice may be summed up in the following two
quotations from the novel *Esaú e Jacob*: "The attentive, truly rumina-
tive reader has four stomachs in his brain, and through these he passes
and repasses the actions and events, until he deduces the truth which
was, or seemed to be, hidden [chap. lv]." "Explanations eat up time
and paper, delay the action, and end by boring. The best thing is to
read with attention [chap. v]."

⁶ E.g., José Veríssimo, *História da Literatura Brasileira* (3d ed.; Rio,
1929), pp. 427–428; Afrânio Coutinho, *A Filosofia de Machado de Assis*
(Rio, Vecchi, 1940), p. 155; Barreto Filho, *Introdução a Machado de
Assis*, pp. 55, 195–197; Augusto Meyer, *À Sombra da Estante* (Rio,
Olympio, 1947), pp. 45–61; José de Mesquita, "De Lívia a Dona
Carmo," *Machado de Assis: Estudos e Ensaios*, ed. Federação das
Academias de Letras do Brasil (Rio, 1940), pp. 15, 28.

CHAPTER 1.

¹ Samuel Putnam, *Marvelous Journey: A Survey of Four Centuries
of Brazilian Writing* (New York, Knopf, 1948), calls Machado de
Assis (p. viii) "one of the great writers of all time," and (p. 17) "a
novelist with whom we have none to compare." Cf. *ibid.*, pp. 37, 178,
182–183. Arturo Torres-Ríoseco, *New World Literature* (Berkeley
and Los Angeles, University of California Press, 1949), p. 208, states:
"As a novelist and writer of short stories, he admits of no peers either
in Spanish or in his own language." Cf. Manuel de Oliveira Lima,
"Machado de Assis et Son Œuvre Littéraire," in *Machado de Assis
et Son Œuvre Littéraire* (Paris, Michaud, 1909), p. 24; Mário de
Andrade, *O Empalhador de Passarinho: Obras Completas XX* (São
Paulo, Martins [1946]), pp. 29–30, 33; José Lins do Rego, *Conferências
no Prata* (Rio, C.E.B., 1946), pp. 36–37, 38.

For Machado de Assis's place in Brazilian letters, see: William F.
Lamont, "The Nobel Prizes in Literature," *Books Abroad*, Vol. XXV,
No. 1 (Winter, 1951), p. 14; Francisco de Assis Barbosa, "Romance,
Contos, Novelas," *Manual Bibliográfico de Estudos Brasileiros*, ed.
Rubens Borba de Moraes and William Berrien (Rio, Gráfica Editora
Souza, 1949), p. 687; Ronald de Carvalho, *Pequena História da
Literatura Brasileira* (6th ed.; Rio, Briguiet, 1937), p. 317; José-Maria
Belo, *Inteligência do Brasil* (3d ed.; São Paulo, Companhia Editora
Nacional, 1938), p. 68; Álvaro Lins, *Jornal de Crítica: Primeira Série*
(Rio, Olympio, 1941), p. 171; Lúcia Miguel Pereira, "Três Romancis-
tas Regionalistas," in *O Romance Brasileiro de 1752 a 1930*, ed.
Aurélio Buarque de Hollanda (Rio, Cruzeiro, 1952), p. 114; and

Lúcia Miguel Pereira, *História da Literatura Brasileira XII: Prosa de Ficção de 1870 a 1920* (Rio, Olympio, 1950), pp. 11, 16.

As for the place of *Dom Casmurro* among Machado's works, in 1943, 180 Brazilian writers cast their ballots in a poll conducted by a Rio de Janeiro newspaper to determine the ten greatest novelists that the country had produced. Machado de Assis headed the list, and the majority of votes for the best novel went to *Dom Casmurro* (see Samuel Putnam, "Brazilian Literature," *Handbook of Latin American Studies* [1943], p. 396). Cf. Barreto Filho, "Machado de Assis," in *O Romance Brasileiro de 1752 a 1930*, p. 145 (*"Dom Casmurro* é um apogeu que não foi ultrapassado"), and Barreto Filho, *Introdução a Machado de Assis* (Rio, A.G.I.R., 1947), pp. 188, 193, 198.

² "Três Tesouros Perdidos," "A Mulher de Prêto," "O Segrêdo de Augusta," "O Relógio de Ouro," "A Parasita Azul," "Nem Uma Nem Outra," "Sem Olhos," "Papéis Velhos," "Troca de Datas," "A Cartomante."

³ The novels *Resurreição* (chap. ix), *A Mão e a Luva* (chap. ii), *Helena* (chap. xxv), *Quincas Borba* (chaps. xl, lxxv, lxxvii, cxliii), *Memórias Póstumas de Braz Cubas* (chap. xcviii), *Dom Casmurro* (chaps. lxii, lxxii, cxxxv); the tales "Questão de Vaidade," "Astúcias de Marido," "Onda," "Aurora Sem Dia," "Sem Olhos," "Curta História," "O Diplomático"; the play *O Protocolo;* criticism and commentary in *Diário do Rio de Janeiro,* Dec. 16, 1861, and Feb. 7, 1865 (CHRONICAS, I, II); "Conversas com as Mulheres," *Semana Ilustrada* (Rio), June 18, 1865 (CONTOS E CRÔNICAS, pp. 110–111); "Notícia da Atual Literatura Brasileira—Instinto de Nacionalidade," *O Novo Mundo,* New York, March 24, 1873 (CRITICA LITTERARIA); " 'O Primo Basílio (1st article, dated April 16, 1878)' " (CRITICA LITTERARIA); his column "A + B," *Gazeta de Notícias* (Rio), Sept. 12, and Oct. 4, 1886 (DIÁLOGOS E REFLEXÕES DE UM RELOJOEIRO, pp. 24 and 40–41); his column "A Semana," *Gazeta de Notícias, Rio,* Jan. 15, and Oct. 29, 1893, July 28, 1895, Aug. 2 and 9, and Dec. 27, 1896 (A SEMANA, I, II, III); "Rossi—Carta a Salvador de Mendonça," *A Reforma* (Rio), July 20, 1871, republished in Machado de Assis, *Páginas Esquecidas,* ed. Eloy Pontes (Rio, Casa Mandarino [1939]).

According to Joaquim Nabuco (*Escriptos e Discursos Literários* [São Paulo, Companhia Editora Nacional, 1939], pp. 25–33) a taste for *Othello* was awakened in Machado's generation by the Brazilian actor João Caetano dos Santos. This actor first presented his *Othello* in Rio de Janeiro in 1857. The text was a Portuguese verse translation made by the Brazilian poet Domingos José Gonçalves de Magalhães of the French adaptation by Jean-François Ducis. In spite of this "triple pulverization" of Shakespeare, as Nabuco calls it, *Othello* remained João Caetano's most popular role.

Machado de Assis mentions João Caetano many times in his writings. He wrote also about the Italian actors Adelaide Ristori and Rossi, who performed Shakespeare in Rio after Caetano's death.

It would seem that Machado was familiar with Alfred de Vigny's translation of *Othello*, at an early date: in his short story "Onda," published in 1867, he renders Othello's "false as water" (V.ii.132) "pérfida como a onda." Vigny's translation (*Œuvres Complètes/ Théâtre/I*, ed. Baldensperger [Paris, Conard, 1926]) is: "Perfide et légère/Comme l'onde." Even in *Dom Casmurro* one finds what seems to be a trace of the Vigny version. At the beginning of chapter cv, in listing his wife's virtues and faults in the manner of Othello (III.iii.183–186), Santiago includes a fondness for jewels—which does not appear in Shakespeare but *is* in the Vigny list (III.iii):

> Que ma femme aime encor ce que son âge entraine,
> La danse et les concerts, le monde et sa gaîté,
> Qu'elle aime les bijoux, parle avec liberté.

And Machado's use in three of the passages cited above ("Carta a Salvador de Mendonça," *Resurreição*, and *Gazeta de Notícias* for Aug. 2, 1896), of the spelling "Yago" perhaps derives from Vigny, who spells "Iago" in that fashion.

It is possible that the fanfare over Verdi's *Otello* (which had its debut in Naples in 1890, ten years before the publication of *Dom Casmurro*) prompted Machado de Assis to use *Othello* and opera as symbols for Santiago's life; but one finds nothing to suggest any closer relationship between Machado's novel and Verdi's work.

Machado de Assis was no doubt reading Shakespeare in English by 1870, when he made his "paraphrase in verse" "A Morte de Ophelia" (POESIAS COMPLETAS). (It was in this year also that he translated *Oliver Twist* for the *Jornal de Tarde*. He must have known some English as early as 1859, when he made a Portuguese translation of Poe's "Raven" in the meter of the original.) Evidence in his works points to a continued study of Shakespeare in the original. (So far I have come across 225 direct references to Shakespeare, including references to twenty of the plays.)

[4] Quotations from *Dom Casmurro* are taken from the published translation of that novel (New York, Noonday Press, 1953); quotations from Machado de Assis's other works were translated by me for the present study.

[5] In more recent years Portuguese dictionaries have amplified their definition of "casmurro" to include the special meaning given by Santiago.

[6] This was the age of Juliet: for Machado's use of this symbol, see below, this study, chap. 8, note 50.

CHAPTER 2.

[1] E.g., in his preface to the first edition of *Resurreição* and in his 1874 preface to *A Mão e a Luva*.

Lúcia Miguel Pereira (*História da Literatura Brasileira XII: Prosa de Ficção de 1870 a 1920* [Rio, Olympio, 1950], p. 102) is of the opinion that Machado de Assis broke his rule in *Dom Casmurro*, and had recourse to a fortuitous circumstance, the resemblance of Ezekiel to Escobar.

[2] *O Cruzeiro*, April 16 and 30, 1878 (CRITICA LITTERARIA).

[3] *Othello*, I.i.58. Unless otherwise stated, all Shakespeare references are to *The Complete Works of William Shakespeare*, ed. W. J. Craig (London, Oxford University Press, 1943).

[4] *Dom Casmurro*, chap. lxiii.

[5] *Ibid.*, chap. civ.

[6] *Ibid.*, chap. ciii.

[7] *Othello*, I.i.19–31; I.iii.403–404; II.i.224–234.

[8] *Dom Casmurro*, chap. lvi.

[9] *Ibid.*, chap. xx. Compare Bento's vow of "a thousand paternosters" in this chapter ["Mil, mil, mil"] with that of the miser Sales of the tale "Entre Santos" ["1.000, 1.000, 1.000"].

[10] *Ibid.*, chaps. lxvii and lxix.

[11] *Ibid.*, chap. civ.

[12] *Ibid.*, chap. cxiv.

[13] *Ibid.*, chap. xci.

[14] *Ibid.*, chap. lxxx.

[15] *Ibid.*, chap. xciv.

[16] *Ibid.*, chap. cvi.

[17] *Ibid.*, chap. cv.

[18] *Ibid.*, chap. lxxxiv.

[19] *Ibid.*, chap. cxxxiv.

[20] *Ibid.*, chap. cxl.

[21] *Ibid.*, chap. cviii.

[22] *Ibid.*, chaps. xviii, xxxi, xlii.

[23] *Ibid.*, chap. cxxxii.

[24] *Ibid.*, chap. xxxviii.

[25] *Ibid.*, chap. xii.

[26] *Ibid.*, chap. xlii.

[27] C. M. Bowra, *Sophoclean Tragedy* (Oxford, Clarendon Press, 1944), p. 368. Cf. D. G. James, *The Dream of Learning* (Oxford, Clarendon Press, 1951, p. 86.

[28] E.g., Paul N. Siegel, "The Damnation of Othello," *Publications of the Modern Language Association of America*, LXVIII (Dec., 1953), 1070–1071.

[29] *Dom Casmurro*, chap. lxviii.

CHAPTER 3.

[1] *Resurreição*, chap. vii.

[2] *Ibid.*, chap. ix.

[3] *Ibid.*, chap. xii.

[4] *Ibid.*, chap. v.

[5] *Ibid.*, chap. xx.

[6] *Ibid.*, chaps. ix, xx.

[7] *Ibid.*, chap. ix.

[8] *Ibid.*, chap. xxii.

[9] *Ibid.*, chap. xxiii.

[10] *Ibid.*, chaps. iv, ix, xi.

[11] *Ibid.*, chap. xi.

[12] *Ibid.*, chaps. vi, vii.

[13] *Ibid.*, chaps. xv, xix.

[14] *Dom Casmurro*, chap. lxxx.

[15] *Ibid.*, chap. lxxix, and passim.

[16] *Ibid.*, chap. xli.

[17] *Esaú e Jacob*, chap. xv. And compare Machado's comment on Benta Hora, who thought himself an emissary of Jesus Christ, and on the bandit Puga, who thought himself to be Jesus Christ, as expressed in the column "A Semana," *Gazeta de Notícias*, Sept. 13, 1896, and Dec. 30, 1894, respectively (A SEMANA, III and II). Finally, one must consider Santiago's remark (*Dom Casmurro*, chap. lxxx), "My name was between the two women like the watchword of the life to come."

[18] E.g., *Dom Casmurro*, chaps. xxv, and xcix ("Woman, behold thy son!").

[19] *Ibid.*, chaps. lxxviii–lxxix, xciii.

[20] *Ibid.*, chap. xxxix.

[21] *Ibid.*, chaps. xv, xxxiv.

[22] *Ibid.*, chap. li.

[23] *Ibid.*, chap. xxv.

[24] *Ibid.*, chaps. xxxii and xliii; cf. chap. cxxiii. Compare Felix of *Resurreição*, who felt himself drawn into the "abyss" of Livia's love (*Resurreição*, chap. viii).

[25] See, for example, his poems "Uma Ode de Anacreonte" and "Versos a Corinna: As Águas" (POESIAS COMPLETAS); the play *Os Deuses de Casaca*, Scene III (THEATRO); "Cartas Fluminenses: Carta à Hetaira," *Diário do Rio de Janeiro*, March 12, 1867 (CHRONICAS, II).

[26] Specifically in *Dom Casmurro*, chaps. lxxx and cvi.

CHAPTER 4.

[1] That Fernão Mendes Pinto symbolized this sort of thing to Machado de Assis is clear from the title of his tale satirizing the will to believe, "O Segrêdo do Bonzo: Capítulo Inédito de Fernão Mendes Pinto": the narrator of this story is Fernão Mendes Pinto, the style is a burlesque of that of Fernão Mendes Pinto.

[2] *Memórias Póstumas de Braz Cubas*, chap. xxxiii.

[3] Letters of Mário de Alencar to Machado de Assis, dated Dec. 16, 1907, and Feb. 20, 1908; Assis to Alencar, Dec. 22, 1907, and Feb. 8, 1908; also letter of José Veríssimo, dated July 18, 1908, and Machado's reply, July 19, 1908 (CORRESPONDENCIA).

[4] "A Mulher de Prêto."

[5] Psalms 52:8.

[6] *Compêndio da Doutrina Cristã*, Liv. 2, as quoted by Domingos Vieira, *Grande Dicionário Português ou Tesouro da Língua Portuguesa* (Porto, Chardron e Moraes, 1878), under "oliveira."

[7] See the farce *Clerigo da Beyra*, lines 16–19.

[8] "A Semana," *Gazeta de Notícias* (Rio), Jan. 10, 1897 (A SEMANA, III).

[9] "A Semana," April 1, 1894 (A SEMANA, II).

[10] *Ibid.*, May 27, 1894.

[11] Edgar Prestage, "Foreword," *Portuguese Voyages 1498—1663*, ed. Charles David Ley (Everyman ed.; London and New York, 1947), p. v.

[12] "Ao Acaso," *Diário do Rio de Janiero*, April 4, 1865 (CHRONICAS, II).

[13] *Memórias Póstumas de Braz Cubas*, chap. iii. Cf. the imaginary Bentos of Machado de Assis's journalism "Badaladas," *Semana Ilustrada*, Dec. 29, 1872, and "História dos Quinze Dias," *Ilustração Brasileira*, Oct. 15, 1876 (both in CHRONICAS, III), and Frei Bento of the apologue "Adão e Eva."

[14] *Os Lusíadas*, I. 14.

[15] "Notas de Leitura de Machado de Assis," *Revista da Academia Brasileira de Letras*, I (1910), 144.

[16] *Os Lusíadas*, V. 9.

[17] *Da Asia* de João de Barros e de Diogo de Couto (Nova ed.; Lisboa, Na Régia Oficina Tipográfica, 1778), Vol. II, Década I.vii.2, p. 93.

[18] As seen, for example, in the explanation of the Negro Prudêncio's treatment of his slave (*Memórias Póstumas de Braz Cubas*, chap. lxviii) or in the discussion of slavery by Helena and Estácio (*Helena*, chap. vi).

[19] Gilberto Freyre, *Casa-Grande e Senzala* (4th ed.; Rio, Olympio, 1943), vol. 1, p. 19.

[20] The short story "Curta História," and the novel *Quincas Borba* (chap. xl).

[21] See, for example: G. Wilson Knight, *Principles of Shakespearian Production* (Harmsworth, Middlesex, Penguin Books, 1949), p. 108; Paul N. Siegel, "The Damnation of Othello," *Publications of the Modern Language Association of America*, LXVIII (1953), 1068–1078.

[22] *Dom Casmurro*, chap. lvi.

[23] In the novels, there are, besides José Dias of *Dom Casmurro*, Agostinho José dos Santos of *Esaú e Jacob*, José da Costa Marcondes Ayres and his servant José who appear in both *Esaú e Jacob* and *Memorial de Ayres;* in the short stories, José de Menezes ("Casada e Viúva"), José Durval ("Cinco Mulheres"), José Brito ("O Segrêdo de Augusta"), José Pires ("Luiz Soares"), José Lemos and José Porfírio ("As Bodas de Luiz Duarte"), the servant of Captain Ferreira ("Nem Uma Nem Outra"), José Mendonça ("Os Óculos de Pedro Antão"), José Mendes ("O Astrólogo"), José Marques ("Um Almôço"), José S. P. Vargas ("Silvestre"), the nephew of Barbosa ("A Melhor das Noivas"), José Cândido ("Um Ambicioso"), José Borges ("Conversão de um Avaro"), José Ribeiro ("Primas de Sapucaia!"), José Maria ("A Segunda Vida"), Procópio José Gomes Vallongo ("O Enfermeiro"), José Martins de Brito ("Anecdota do Cabriolet"), José Martins ("Umas Férias").

[24] José Rodrigues, passim *Gazeta de Notícias*, 1892–1896 (A SEMANA, I, II, III). This character supplants "meu moleque" of earlier columns (CHRONICAS, I, II, III, IV).

[25] José Cândido of the short story "Um Ambicioso."

[26] *Esaú e Jacob*, chap. lxxxi.

[27] The other six are found in *Dom Casmurro*, and in the short stories "O Anjo Rafael," "Nem Uma Nem Outra," "O Bote de Rapé," "A Chave," "O Enfermeiro."

[28] *Esaú e Jacob*, chap. xxxviii.

[29] D. P. Kidder and J. C. Fletcher, *Brazil and the Brazilians* (Philadelphia, Childs & Peterson, 1857), pp. 124, 172, 326, 332.

[30] With the exception perhaps of Ayres, who served as "spiritual father" to the twins (*Esaú e Jacob*, chaps. xxxviii, xliv).

[31] E.g., in "Phalenas: Pálida Elvira xxx" (POESIAS COMPLETAS); criticism of Luiz Guimarães Junior's *O Lírio Branco* in *O Futuro* (Rio), Jan. 1, 1863 (CHRONICAS, I)—where "clear, blue horizon" is equated with "pure young love." Cf.: "the blue soul of Juliet"—"Último Capítulo" (HISTORIAS SEM DATA); Natividade, who still had a "blue soul" at forty because she had passed through life "intact and pure"— *Esaú e Jacob*, chap. xix; *Dom Casmurro*, chaps. lxxx–lxxxi (Capitú), and chap. xciii (Escobar and Bento). Cf. Machado de Assis's letter to Lúcio de Mendonça, Jan. 24, 1872 (CORRESPONDENCIA): "But why clouds? You don't have any at your age—which is rather a time of clear, blue sky, enthusiasm, rapture, and faith."

[32] *Esaú e Jacob*, chap. xix. The symbolism is taken from Camões's story of Adamastor and Thetis (*Os Lusíadas*, V).

[33] "Ao Acaso," *Diário do Rio de Janeiro*, Jan. 31, 1865 (CHRONICAS, II).

[34] Particularly in his tale "A Sereníssima República," which he explains in a note as an allegorical account of Brazilian election practices. Cf. his columns of May 12, 1864, and of Oct. 15, 1876, in *Semana Ilustrada* (CHRONICAS, I and III, respectively); *Esaú e Jacob*, chap. xxxvi. The symbolism is superficially appropriate because "sereníssimo" and "sereníssima" were used as titles of members of the House of Bragança: Machado, in his columns, refers to Pedro II's daughters as the "sereníssimas princesas."

[35] An earlier version of matter covered in *Dom Casmurro*, chaps. iii, iv, and v, which appeared in *A República* (Rio), Nov. 15, 1896, under the title "Um Agregado (Capítulo de um Livro Inédito)," has been republished in CONTOS ESPARSOS, pp. 269–273. In this earlier version, all but one of the characters mentioned have the same names as in the novel: Dona Maria da Gloria, Bentinho, Uncle Cosme, Cousin Justina, José Dias, are the same; but Padua appears under the name Fialho. And his daughter, who is not named, is thirteen years old, instead of fourteen, as in *Dom Casmurro*: for Machado de Assis and "the age of Juliet," see below, this study, note 50 to chap. 8.

[36] *Dom Casmurro*, chap. cv.

[37] *Resurreição*, chap. iii.

[38] *Dom Casmurro*, chap. lxxxiii: "her mouth [had] a new imperium."

[39] Both letters dated March 2 (without indication of year, but written during his courtship of Carolina), are published in *Exposição Machado de Assis: Centenário do Nascimento de Machado de Assis: 1839–1939*, ed. Instituto Nacional do Livro (Rio, 1939), pp. 62–64.

[40] *Ibid.*, p. 178.

[41] *Ibid.*, p. 136.

[42] Namely Carmo, Rita, and Fidélia, of *Memorial de Ayres*. Lúcia Miguel Pereira (*Machado de Assis: Estudo Crítico e Biográfico* [5th ed.; Rio, Olympio, 1955], p. 272) notes that the characters Ayres and Aguiar, of the same novel, represent two facets of Machado de Assis himself; and Barreto Filho ("Machado de Assis," *O Romance Brasileiro de 1752 a 1930*, ed. Aurélio Buarque de Hollanda [Rio, Cruzeiro, 1952], p. 148) develops this theme. In the same way, I believe, but to a greater degree, Carmo, Rita, and Fidélia represent three aspects of Carolina mentioned by Eloy Pontes (*A Vida Contraditória de Machado de Assis* [Rio, Olympio, 1939], pp. 163, 182–184), "mother," "sister," "wife." Further, I believe, these three women portray Carolina at various ages and under varying (hypothetical) conditions: Carmo, the actual Carolina in later life as Machado's wife; Fidélia, the young Carolina who defied her family to marry Machado, with the addition of the Carolina that would have been, had Machado died before her, in his youth; Rita, what Carolina would have been if Machado had died first, but in middle age.

It is this identity of Carmo and Fidélia, I believe, which accounts for Machado de Assis's almost constant confusion of their names in his manuscript—a fact which has been adverted to by Lúcia Miguel Pereira (*ibid.*, pp. 272–273) and by Peregrino Junior (*Doença e Constituição de Machado de Assis* [Rio, Olympio, 1938], pp. 143–153), though their explanations are quite different from each other's, and from mine.

[43] *Exposição Machado de Assis*, pp. 202–206 (letters of Machado de Assis to his publisher H. Garnier, Paris, and to the publisher's agent at Rio de Janeiro, J. Lansac: Feb. 12, 1900 [Garnier], Sept. 8, 1902, and July 10, 1903 [Lansac], Nov. 9, 1903, and an undated letter concerning *Memorial de Ayres* [Garnier]).

[44] *Ibid.*, pp. 100, 119.

[45] *Dom Casmurro*, chap. xxxvii.

[46] *Ibid.*, chap. cxlii.

[47] *Ibid.*, chap. xxi.

There is a Justina in one of Machado de Assis's short stories ("Ernesto de Tal") who could have been the twin sister of Santiago's cousin—if indeed she was not the same woman in girlhood.

[48] *Dom Casmurro*, chap. cxvii.

[49] "Aí está o caso em que nem o mais fino Escobar era capaz de resolver...." Machado de Assis in *Gazeta de Notícias*, Nov. 7, 1883 (CRÔNICAS DE LÉLIO, p. 43).

[50] *Dom Casmurro*, chap. xcvi.

[51] It might be noted that these are the only two places in the text of the book in which there is such alteration of type.

[52] *Dom Casmurro*, chap. cxxix.

[53] One might mention also a contemporary of Machado de Assis, Honório Gurgel, a long-winded city councilman mentioned by Machado in his column in the *Gazeta de Notícias* for July 14, 1895 (A SEMANA, II).

[54] The geographical names must also have a significance. (Cf.

Machado de Assis's fantasy on the "Rua do Pagão," in *Gazeta de Notícias*, Aug. 5, 1894 [A SEMANA, II]). The implication of "Rua de Gloria" has been mentioned in the text of this study (chap. 3); that of "Itaguahy," Bento's birthplace, will be taken up in chap. 10. "Matacavallos," as Machado uses it in this novel, seems to mean "kill-horse," connoting the adverbial expression "a matacavalos" ("hell-for-leather") and to refer to the dandies who raced their horses along this street. It might be noted that in "Um Agregado" (see above, note 35), Dona Gloria's house was on the "Rua do Rezende"; and Bento's birthplace was Cantagallo, not Itaguahy. "Engenho Novo," historically meaning the "new (sugar) mill," seems to include another meaning of *engenho*, that is, "device," and to have reference to Santiago's restoration here of the old house formerly located on Matacavallos Street. Because of ignorance of Rio de Janeiro history and geography, I am unable to offer clues to the significance of other place names.

[55] J. Leite de Vasconcellos, *Antroponimia Portuguesa* (Lisboa, Imprensa Nacional, 1928), pp. 469–470; Simões da Fonseca, *Dicionário Enciclopédico da Língua Portuguesa* (Rio and Paris, Garnier, 1926), "Manduca."

[56] *Dom Casmurro*, chap. xci.

[57] *Ibid.*

[58] *Ibid.*, chap. xx.

[59] J. Leite de Vasconcellos, *Lições de Filologia Portuguesa* (Lisboa, Biblioteca Nacional, 1926), pp. 424–426; Vasconcellos, *Antroponimia*, pp. 77, 82–84.

[60] *Ibid.*, p. 82.

[61] Latin Vulgate. In the English Versions translated from the Greek, these verses are numbered 54 and 56.

[62] "História dos Quinze Dias," *Ilustração Brasileira*, April 1, 1877 (CHRONICAS, III); *Quincas Borba*, chap. i.

Chapter 6.

[1] *Gazeta de Notícias* (Rio), Nov. 15, 1896 (A SEMANA, III).

[2] E.g., Ayres (see prefaces to *Esaú e Jacob* and *Memorial de Ayres*), or Braz Cubas (see *Memórias Póstumas de Braz Cubas*, "Ao Leitor").

[3] E.g., *Dom Casmurro*, chaps. ii, li, lx, lxix.

Chapter 7.

[1] "Introduction," *Shakespeare's Othello*, ed. William J. Rolfe (New York, American Book Company, 1903), p. 16.

[2] *Dom Casmurro*, chap. cxlv.

[3] *Ibid.*, chap. cxlvii.

[4] *Ibid.*, chap. cxii.

[5] D. P. Kidder and J. C. Fletcher, *Brazil and the Brazilians* (Philadelphia, Childs & Peterson, 1857), p. 166; Gilberto Freyre, *Casa-Grande e Senzala* (4th ed.; Rio, Olympio, 1943), vol. 1, pp. 364–

183

PENNSYLVANIA MILITARY COLLEGE
CHESTER, PENNSYLVANIA
LIBRARY

366; Charles Expilly, *Mulheres e Costumes do Brasil,* trans. Gastão Penalva (São Paulo, Companhia Editora Nacional, 1935), pp. 400–405.

[6] Yet does not the episode of the barber (chap. cxxvii) imply that it was Santiago who was practising an art, and the barber's playing symbolize Santiago's fabrication of the evil he attributes to Capitú? ("As for the husband, he was now playing with fervor. He did not see his wife, he did not see his customers. He glued his face to the instrument, his soul passed into the bow, and he played and played . . . Divine art!")

[7] *Dom Casmurro,* chap. lix.

[8] Cf. the attitude of Livia (*Resurreição*).

[9] José Veríssimo, *Estudos de Literatura Brasileira: Terceira Série* (Rio, Garnier, 1903), p. 44.

[10] *Dom Casmurro,* chaps. cxv–cxvi.

[11] *Ibid.,* chaps. cxvi, cxlv.

[12] *Ibid.,* chap. cxxxi.

[13] *Ibid.,* chap. lxxxiii.

[14] *Ibid.,* chap. cxl.

[15] *Ibid.,* chaps. v, vii, xxxi.

[16] *Ibid.,* chap. xxxiii.

[17] *Ibid.,* chap. lii.

[18] *Ibid.,* chaps. xxv, xxxiv, and passim.

[19] *Ibid.,* chap. xcix.

[20] *Ibid.,* chap. cxxxi.

[21] *Esaú e Jacob,* chap. xxix.

[22] *Quincas Borba,* chap. cvi. Cf. *Dom Casmurro,* chap. li: ". . . the evil is rather in your own perverse head than in that of those two adolescents."

[23] Like Leontes in *The Winter's Tale.*

[24] *Dom Casmurro,* chap. xii.

[25] *Ibid.,* chap. xxxviii.

[26] *Ibid.,* chap. xiv.

[27] *Ibid.,* chap. lxxx.

[28] *Ibid.,* chap. xlix.

[29] *Ibid.,* chap. cvi.

[30] *Ibid.,* chaps. lxxx, cvi.

[31] In particular, *ibid.,* chap. lxvii, in which Capitú glories in Bento's anguish over his mother's illness.

[32] *Ibid.,* chap. cxv.

[33] *Ibid.,* chap. cix.

[34] *Ibid.,* chaps. xv, xxxiv, xxxviii, lxxxiii.

[35] *Ibid.,* chap. xviii.

[36] *Ibid.,* chap. cxl.

Chapter 8.

[1] *Dom Casmurro,* chap. lvi.

[2] Cf. *ibid.,* chap. cvii: "My fits of jealousy were intense but brief: in an instant I would tear down everything, but in the same instant

I would reconstruct the sky, the earth, and the stars." Santiago was already handy at demolition and reconstruction.

3 *Ibid.,* chap. lix.

4 Twice in chapter ii, and once each in chapters xxxi and cxlv.

5 *Ibid.,* chap. xxxi.

6 See in particular Act V of Corneille's *Sophonisbe,* a likely source of Machado's knowledge of this story.

7 *Dom Casmurro,* chap. cxlv.

8 Cf. Machado's short story "O Capitão Mendonça" (CONTOS RECOLHIDOS, p. 177): "'O amor é quase tudo na vida . . . As grandezas da terra não valem uma flor nascida à beira dos rios.'"

9 F. J. Caldas Aulete, *Dicionário Contemporâneo da Língua Portuguesa* (Lisboa, 1881).

10 Rendered in the English translation "a darling."

11 Cf. Santiago's description of his dream house (chap. xlix): "I planted flowers round it."

12 E.g.: The worm (jealousy) kills the flower (the heart) filled with dewy perfume from heaven (love) and planted by a god ("Phalenas: O Verme" [POESIAS COMPLETAS]). "Cynicism . . . can spoil an upright, pure, and lofty conscience in the same way the bookworm can gnaw the most sublime books in the world ("Balas de Estalo 1884–1885," *Gazeta de Notícias* [CHRONICAS, IV]). "Death is a worm, of two sorts according as it enters the body or the soul. It kills in both cases." ("Sem Olhos" [RELIQUIAS DE CASA VELHA, II]).

13 Cf. "Phalenas Uma Ode de Anacreonte" (POESIAS COMPLETAS), where the lance of Achilles is "Love"—"As feridas que faz o mesmo Amor as cura; / Brandem armas iguais Achilles e Cupido."

14 Machado de Assis's foreword to *Helena; Memórias Póstumas de Braz Cubas,* chaps. xxvii and xxxviii; and the above quotation (note 12) from "Balas de Estalo."

15 In Padre Pereira's Portuguese translation of the Vulgate this passage (Mark 8:35–36) is the same as the English Version, with the Latin word "anima" rendered as "vida" ("life"). But in the parallel passage (Matt. 16:25–26) the Portuguese translation renders the word "anima" as "alma" ("soul"), so that an English translation of the Portuguese translation would read: "For whosoever would save his soul shall lose it: and whosoever shall lose his soul for love of me shall find it. For what is a man profited if he shall gain the whole world and lose his own soul?" This passage thus makes clear the other horn of Bento's dilemma: in choosing to save his soul by becoming a priest, instead of losing his soul by loving Capitú, he would lose his soul. Santiago fell between the horns.

16 *Dom Casmurro,* chap. lxiv.

17 *Ibid.,* chap. xv.

18 E.g., "Occidentais: Uma Creatura" and "Phalenas: Manhã de Inverno" (POESIAS COMPLETAS); *Memórias Póstumas de Braz Cubas,* chaps. vii, lvii; *Esaú e Jacob,* chap. i: the "destiny" of the fortuneteller Barbara is equated with "nature" by the posy "Dico che quando l'anima mal nata... Dante."

185

[19] *Dom Casmurro,* chap. vii.

[20] *Ibid.,* chap. vi.

[21] *Ibid.,* chaps. lxxi–lxxiii.

[22] *Ibid.,* chap. cxxxii.

[23] Cf. Machado's column in *Gazeta de Notícias,* Dec. 30, 1894 (A SEMANA, II), in which "Shakespeare gave way to Lynch [i.e., to the evil in the natures of the mob]" in the writing of the tragedy of the bandit Puga.

[24] *Dom Casmurro,* chap. x.

[25] *Ibid.,* chap. lxvii.

[26] *Ibid.,* chap. cxviii.

[27] *Ibid.,* chap. xiv.

[28] *Ibid.,* chap. xxxii.

[29] *Ibid.,* chap. xlvi.

[30] *Ibid.,* chap. li.

[31] *Ibid.,* chap. xcv.

[32] *Ibid.,* chap. ci.

[33] *Ibid.,* chap. xcviii.

[34] For the same figure, see *A Mão e a Luva,* chap. xv; and "Phalenas: A um Legista" (POESIAS COMPLETAS)—

> Rosa... que se enamora
> Do amante colibrí
>
> . . . . . .
>
> Mas Zephyro bregeiro
> Opõe ao beija-flor
> Embargos de terceiro
> Senhor e possuidor.

[35] *Dom Casmurro,* chap. cxxii.

[36] *Ibid.,* chap. cvi.

[37] *Ibid.,* chap. xxv.

[38] *Ibid.,* chaps. xlix, cxxxii.

[39] *Ibid.,* chap. cv.

[40] *Ibid.,* chaps. cvi, cvii.

[41] *Ibid.,* chap. cviii.

[42] *Ibid.,* chap. cxvii.

[43] *Ibid.,* chap. cxviii.

[44] *Ibid.,* chap. cxviii.

[45] *Ibid.,* chap. cxxi.

[46] *Ibid.,* chap. cxxiii.

[47] *Ibid.,* chap. cxxxv.

[48] *Ibid.,* chap. cxxxii.

[49] *Ibid.,* chap. cxvii.

[50] *Dom Casmurro,* chaps. lxxx–lxxxi.

As noted above (chaps. 1 and 7), Capitú was the age of Juliet. Machado de Assis used "the age of Juliet" interchangeably with these other symbols: for example, in the short story "O Anjo das Donzelas": ". . . the age of Juliet; it is the flower, it is life, it is hope, blue sky, green fields . . . dawn breaking . . ." Cf. above, this study, chap. 1, note 6; chap. 4, notes 31 and 35.

[51] *Ibid.,* chaps. xciii, cxliii.

[52] *Ibid.,* chap. lix. Cf. "Bons Dias!" for Aug. 22, 1889 (DIALOGOS E REFLEXÕES DE UM RELOJOEIRO, p. 263); also see Shakespeare's *The Winter's Tale,* II.iii.103–107, and *Much Ado About Nothing,* II.i.305–308.

[53] *Dom Casmurro,* chap. xii.

[54] *Ibid.,* chap. lxxxv.

[55] *Ibid.,* chap. cxliv.

[56] Cf. *Esaú e Jacob,* chap. xlii, where Ayres's regrets are called "swallows"; also "Phalenas: Pássaros" (Machado compares his sad thoughts to swallows); "Americanas: A Cristã Nova v" ("thought is like birds of passage"); "A Gonçalves Dias" (bird of death); "Os Orizes" and note by Machado de Assis (the owl is a "living symbol of avenging time"). (All the foregoing poems are to be found in POESIAS COMPLETAS.) Cf. Machado's frequent use of Chateaubriand's "cranes," as in *Memórias Póstumas de Braz Cubas,* chaps. i and v, and in *Gazeta de Notícias,* Nov. 15, 1896 (A SEMANA, III).

[57] *Dom Casmurro,* chap. cxliv.

[58] In "Um Agregado" (CONTOS ESPARSOS, pp. 269–273), described above (this study, note 35 to chap. 4), the wording on the life within and without Dona Gloria's house is a little less subtle than in the final version. In "Um Agregado," ". . . life [inside the house] like the house was monotonous and gloomy [monótona e soturna] . . . Life outside was gay, intense, and varied [festiva, intensa, e variada]." Dom Casmurro says of his reproduction of his mother's house, "And now, as formerly, there is the same contrast between the life within, which is tranquil [pacata], and that without, which is noisy and restless [ruidosa]."

[59] *Dom Casmurro,* chap. xxvi.

[60] *Ibid.,* chap. xv.

[61] *Ibid.,* chap. xlvii.

[62] *Ibid.,* chap. cxl.

[63] *Ibid.,* chap. cxxxiii.

[64] *Ibid.,* chap. lxvii.

[65] *Ibid.,* chaps. xxx, lxxxiv, lxxxvi.

[66] *Ibid.,* chap. lxviii.

[67] *Ibid.,* chap. lxxxiii.

[68] *Ibid.,* chaps. xxii, lxvi, cxxxiv.

[69] *Ibid.,* chap. vii.

[70] *Ibid.,* chap. cxl.

[71] *Ibid.,* chap. lxxv.

[72] Cf. *Memórias Póstumas de Braz Cubas,* chap. lxiv, for this idea that forgetting a loved object is a way of killing it.

[73] Thus there is a parallelism between the "bird of death" wish emerging from his brain and the submerged Casmurro breaking through into the open.

[74] *Dom Casmurro,* chap. cxxxiv.

[75] Cf. *ibid.,* chap. cvii: "in an instant I would tear down everything . . ."

[76] *Memórias Póstumas de Braz Cubas,* chap. vi.
[77] *Dom Casmurro,* chap. xcii.
[78] *Ibid.,* chaps. civ, cxiv, cxviii.

CHAPTER 9.

[1] E.g., *Memórias Póstumas de Braz Cubas,* chap. vii; "Occidentais: Uma Creatura" (POESIAS COMPLETAS). (In this poem, not only is death a part of life; life is equated with love, and death with self-love.)
Machado's use of the tree as a symbol of life, with birds (forms of death) living in its branches, again images the idea that death is a part of life.
[2] *Dom Casmurro,* chap. xxxvii.
[3] "Americanas: A Cristã Nova" (POESIAS COMPLETAS).
[4] *Esaú e Jacob,* chap. xxix.
[5] *Dom Casmurro,* chap. cxxxviii.
[6] "Phalenas" (POESIAS COMPLETAS).
[7] *Gazeta de Notícias* (Rio), March 8, 1896 (A SEMANA, III). Cf. "Occidentais: O Desfecho" (POESIAS COMPLETAS).
[8] Letter to José Veríssimo, Jan. 5, 1900 (CORRESPONDENCIA).
[9] "Ao Acaso," *Diário do Rio de Janeiro,* July 10, 1864 (CHRONICAS, II). Cf. Machado de Assis, *Adelaide Ristori: Folhetins* (Rio, Academia Brasileira de Letras, 1955), pp. 20–21, 46.
[10] *Dom Casmurro,* chap. cxxv.
[11] *Resurreição,* chap. i.
[12] Ayres's entry for Sept. 4, 1888. Ayres remarks throughout on her persistence.
[13] *The Merchant of Venice,* III.v.44–47; *Titus Andronicus,* IV.ii.-51–54.
[14] C. M. Bowra, *Sophoclean Tragedy* (Oxford, Clarendon Press, 1944), p. 359. It might be added that the whole plot development in *Dom Casmurro* is Sophoclean: cf. Bowra, *op. cit.,* p. 15, "As the drama develops, the nature of the problem becomes clearer, and eventually we know what it is." Cf. Barreto Filho, *Introdução a Machado de Assis* (Rio, A.G.I.R., 1947), p. 194.
[15] "A. Semana," *Gazeta de Notícias,* July 28, 1895 (A SEMANA, II).

CHAPTER 10.

[1] *Esaú e Jacob,* chap. xxviii.
[2] "A Semana," *Gazeta de Notícias* (Rio), July 14, 1895 (A SEMANA, II).
[3] "A Semana," *Gazeta de Notícias,* Aug. 6, 1893 (A SEMANA, I).
[4] *Diário do Rio de Janeiro,* Sept. 5, 1864 (CHRONICAS, II).
[5] "A. Semana," *Gazeta de Notícias,* Dec. 29, 1895 (A SEMANA, III).
[6] *Dom Casmurro,* chap. cxl. Cf. G. Wilson Knight, *Principles of Shakespearian Production* (Harmsworth, Middlesex, Penguin Books,

1949), p. 125; and H. D. F. Kitto, *Form and Meaning in Drama* (London, Methuen, 1956), chap. 9.

⁷ E.g., *Dom Casmurro*, chap. cviii.

⁸ *Ibid.*, chap. lxviii.

⁹ E.g., Harold C. Goddard, *The Meaning of Shakespeare* (Chicago, University of Chicago Press, 1954), pp. 455–457, 500; G. Wilson Knight, "Myth and Miracle," in his *The Crown of Life* (London, Methuen, 1948), pp. 10–11, 20.

As early as 1866 Machado de Assis fused Othello and Hamlet, but for comic purposes, in the short story "Astúcias de Marido" ("Desde então a questão de Otelo entrou no espírito de Valentim e fez cama aí: ser ou não ser amado, tal era o problema").

¹⁰ In "A Semana," *Gazeta de Notícias*, Nov. 25, 1894 (A SEMANA, II), Machado cites Caldas Aulete as an authority for the spelling *"pique-nique."*

¹¹ *Quincas Borba*, chap. xl. Cf. Machado's column "Ao Acaso," *Diário do Rio de Janeiro*, Jan. 31, 1865 (CHRONICAS, II): "O diabo cortou as pontas e lançou a cauda ao fogo . . ."

¹² E.g.: *Othello*, I.iii.409–410; II.iii.359–362.

¹³ "A Semana," *Gazeta de Notícias*, Nov. 15, 1896 (A SEMANA, III).

¹⁴ "O Caso Ferrari," *O Cruzeiro* (Rio), May 21, 1878 (CRITICA THEATRAL).

¹⁵ L. C. Knights, *Explorations* (London, Chatto & Windus, 1946), pp. 18–19.

¹⁶ *Dom Casmurro*, chap. lv.

¹⁷ *Ibid.*, chap. c.

¹⁸ *Ibid.*, chaps. xxxi, lxvii–lxviii, xci, cxiv.

¹⁹ *Ibid.*, chaps. cxxxiii–cxxxiv.

²⁰ Kenneth O. Myrick, "The Theme of Damnation in Shakespearean Tragedy," *Studies in Philology*, XXXVIII (1941), 235–245; cf. S. L. Bethell, "Shakespeare's Imagery: The Diabolic Images in *Othello*," *Shakespeare Survey 5* (London, Cambridge University Press, 1952), pp. 71–72.

²¹ Goddard, *The Meaning of Shakespeare*, p. 496; Kenneth Muir, "Introduction," Arden ed. of *Macbeth* (London, Methuen, 1953), pp. l–li.

²² G. Wilson Knight, *The Crown of Life*, pp. 10–11.

²³ For the unity of Shakespeare, see in particular T. S. Eliot's essay on John Ford in his *Selected Essays* (New York, Harcourt, 1950), pp. 170–180.

²⁴ *Romeo and Juliet*, II.ii.133–135; III.v.133. See above, this study, note 50 to chap. 8, for the meaning of Juliet's age in Machado de Assis.

²⁵ *Dom Casmurro*, chap. cii.

²⁶ *Ibid.*, chap. xxxii.

²⁷ *Ibid.*, chaps. xv, xxx, lii.

²⁸ *Othello*, I.iii.164–166.

²⁹ *Dom Casmurro*, chap. cvii.

³⁰ *Ibid.*, chap. cxl.

189

[31] *Ibid.*, chap. cxiii.

[32] *Ibid.*, chap. lxxxi.

[33] Folio reading for *Othello*, III.iii.341.

[34] *Dom Casmurro*, chap. xcix.

[35] E.g., G. Wilson Knight, *The Shakespearian Tempest* (London, Methuen, 1953), pp. 179–183; G. Wilson Knight, *Principles of Shakespearian Production*, pp. 96–97; Goddard, *The Meaning of Shakespeare*, pp. 465–469.

[36] *Dom Casmurro*, chap. cxxxii.

[37] *Ibid.*, chap. cxlv.

[38] *Ibid.*, chap. xliv.

[39] John Money, "Othello's 'It is the Cause . . .' an Analysis," *Shakespeare Survey 6* (London, Cambridge University Press, 1953), pp. 94–105.

[40] E.g., *Dom Casmurro*, chap. xxxiv.

[41] *Ibid.*, chap. lxxv.

[42] *Ibid.*, chap. cxxxv.

[43] *Ibid.*, chaps. lxii, cxxvi, cxxxv.

[44] E.g., he was flattered by José Dias's attentions, by Manduca's eagerness for his arguments, by the comments of people in the street as the chaise went by, by Sancha's and other girls' interest in him; he was vain of his mother's wealth, beauty, and goodness, of Escobar's friendship; he tore down the old house because it did not remember him.

[45] *Dom Casmurro*, chap. xcviii.

[46] *Ibid.*, chap. cxviii.

[47] *Ibid.*, chap. cxxxii.

[48] *Ibid.*, chap. cxlv.

[49] "A Semana," *Gazeta de Notícias* (A SEMANA, I).

[50] Edward S. Dowden, *Shakspere—His Mind and Art* (new ed.; New York and London, Harper, 1918), p. 216.

[51] *Dom Casmurro*, chap. cxl.

[52] *Ibid.*, chap. cxxxv.

[53] *Ibid.*, chap. cxl.

[54] As, for example, in *Resurreição*, already discussed above. Cf. the short story "Questão de Vaidade," part vi: "Ora, a vaidade quando domina o coração do homem . . . não deixa atender a nenhum sentimento mais, a nenhuma razão de justiça."

[55] *Ibid.*; cf. Paul N. Siegel, "The Damnation of Othello," *Publications of the Modern Language Association of America*, LXVIII (Dec., 1953), 1070.

[56] John Money, p. 95.

[57] T. S. Eliot, "Shakespeare and the Stoicism of Seneca," in his *Selected Essays* (New York, Harcourt, 1950), p. 111.

[58] The chapter "Retrospective Exhibition" demonstrates Santiago's compulsion to tell his story and be exonerated; it also shows clearly that none of those women exonerated him.

CHAPTER 11.

[1] *Esaú e Jacob*, chap. xiii; cf. *ibid.*, chap. v.

[2] Cf. *Memorial de Ayres*, "1889—26 de Março," where the narrator, in commenting on the reformed speech and manners of Dona Cesaria, writes: "Deus vencia aquí o diabo com um sorriso tão manso e terno que faria esquecer a existência do imundo sócio."

[3] *Dom Casmurro*, chap. xxix.

[4] *Ibid.*, chap. lv.

[5] Letters of Mário de Alencar to Machado de Assis, dated Dec. 16, 1907, and Feb. 20, 1908; Assis to Alencar, Dec. 22, 1907, and Feb. 8, 1908; also letter of José Veríssimo, dated July 18, 1908, and Machado's reply, July 19, 1908 (CORRESPONDENCIA). Cf. Lúcia Miguel Pereira, *Machado de Assis: Estudo Crítico e Biográfico* (5th ed.; Rio, Olympio, 1955), p. 118; and Barreto Filho, "Machado de Assis," *O Romance Brasileiro de 1752 a 1930*, ed. Aurélio Buarque de Hollanda (Rio, Cruzeiro, 1952), pp. 148–149.

[6] *Memorial de Ayres*, "18 de Setembro de 1888."

[7] Lúcia Miguel Pereira, *Machado de Assis* (5th ed.), pp. 110–112.

[8] *Ibid.*, p. 121; cf. Machado de Assis's letter of Nov. 19, 1869, to Ramos Paz, *Exposição Machado de Assis: Centenário do Nascimento de Machado de Assis 1839–1939*, ed. Instituto Nacional do Livro (Rio, 1939), pp. 64 and 82.

[9] Lúcia Miguel Pereira, *Machado de Assis* (5th ed.), p. 254.

[10] *Ibid.*, p. 102; and Barreto Filho, *Introdução a Machado de Assis* (Rio, A.G.I.R., 1947), pp. 13–14; R. Magalhães Junior, *Machado de Assis Desconhecido* (Rio, Editora Civilização, 1955), pp. 96, 132, 162–164.

[11] Letter to Joaquim Nabuco, dated Jan. 14, 1882 (CORRESPONDENCIA); *Exposição Machado de Assis*, p. 96.

It might be noted too that Machado de Assis and Santiago were contemporaries: Santiago was born in 1842, Machado in 1839. And if Santiago's word can be trusted (for his dating is sometimes contradictory), the *Panegyric* was printed in 1856 (chap. liv), that is, two years before Santiago entered the seminary. Thus, it would seem, the anonymous author may well have been a little older than Santiago.

[12] See, for example, his "Secretária de Agricultura," *Gazeta de Notícias* (Rio), Sept. 12, 1890 (POESIA E PROSA), pp. 154–156. See also, p. 79 of the same collection, the comment of the editor, J. Galante de Sousa.

[13] Lúcia Miguel Pereira, *Machado de Assis* (5th ed.), pp. 46–49, 54–56; Alfredo Pujol, *Machado de Assis* (2d. ed.; São Paulo, Levi, 1917), pp. 8–11.

[14] *Quincas Borba*, chap. x.

[15] Machado de Assis, *Casa Velha* (São Paulo, Martins, 1944), chap. iii.

[16] *Dom Casmurro*, chap. vii ("Era filha de uma senhora mineira, descendente de outra paulista, a familia Fernandes").

[17] E.g., Barreto Filho, *Introdução a Machado de Assis*, pp. 17, 116–

117, 144; Barreto Filho, "Machado de Assis," *O Romance Brasileiro de 1752 a 1930*, ed. Aurélio Buarque de Hollanda (Rio, Cruzeiro, 1952), p. 121; Graça Aranha, *Machado de Assis e Joaquim Nabuco* (São Paulo, Monteiro Lobato, 1923), p. 18.

It might be noted that Braz Cubas (*Memórias Póstumas de Braz Cubas*, chap. cxxxi) draws a distinction between a man's and a woman's love. A woman, he says, "gives herself for love's sake": but a large measure of a man's love is made up of vanity. In "A Paixão de Jesus" (DIALOGOS E REFLEXÕES DE UM RELO-JOEIRO, p. 277), Machado himself makes a similar distinction between men and women. After describing the torture and mockery inflicted upon Jesus by the men, he adds, "but there is still wanting one thing to complete the human part of that last scene.

"The women came . . . in a spirit that was mostly lacking in the men, they [the women] brought consolation and patience to the feet of the man on the cross. No egoism kept them away, no fear . . ."

[18] *Dom Casmurro*, chap. lv.

[19] *Ibid.*, chap. lx.

[20] *Ibid.*, chap. lxxix. In this chapter Santiago seems to be talking about his mother. But he previously stated (chaps. lvi–lxi) that this whole section of his narrative was a part of the panegyric; even in this chapter (lxxix) and the two following, his stressing of his authorship makes it clear that he has his own panegyric in mind.

[21] *Esaú e Jacob*, chaps. v–vi. Cf. *Quincas Borba*, chap. cvi.

[22] E.g., "A Semana," *Gazeta de Notícias*, Feb. 26, 1893, and Aug. 9, 1896 (A SEMANA, I, III); and the short story "Suje-se Gordo!".

[23] G. Wilson Knight, *Principles of Shakespearian Production* (Harmsworth, Middlesex, Penguin Books, 1949), p. 34.

[24] Cf. Kenneth Muir, "Introduction," Arden edition of *King Lear* (London, Methuen, 1952), pp. lv–lx, where he states that *King Lear* "is not, as some of our grandfathers believed, pessimistic and pagan," but is rather an attempt to show that what man needs for happiness in life is "patience, stoical fortitude, and love," and, above all, mutual forgiveness and charity.

[25] "Notas Semanais iv," *O Cruzeiro*, June 2, 1878 (CHRONICAS, IV).

CHAPTER 12.

[1] José Veríssimo, *Estudos de Literatura Brasileira: Primeira Série 1895–1898* (Rio, Garnier, 1901), pp. 253–254; José Veríssimo, *Estudos de Literatura Brasileira: Sexta Série* (Rio, Garnier, 1907), p. 215.

[2] Letter to José Veríssimo, Dec. 15, 1898 (CORRESPONDENCIA); Machado's foreword to the 1905 edition of *Helena* and to the 1907 edition of *A Mão e a Luva;* letter to his publisher H. Garnier, dated Oct. 30, 1899, and printed in *Exposição Machado de Assis: Centenário do Nascimento de Machado de Assis 1839–1939*, ed. Instituto Nacional do Livro (Rio, 1939), pp. 200–201. Cf. Barreto Filho, *Introdução a Machado de Assis* (Rio, A.G.I.R., 1947), pp. 47–48, 59–62.

[8] Published by Paula Brito in 1861 (reprinted in CHRONICAS, I). For convincing proof that this is an original work of Machado de Assis's, rather than a translation, as formerly supposed, see Lúcia Miguel Pereira, *Machado de Assis: Estudo Crítico e Biográfico* (5th ed.; Rio, Olympio, 1955), pp. 90–94; and J. Galante de Sousa, *Bibliografia de Machado de Assis* (Rio, Instituto Nacional do Livro, 1955), pp. 340–342.

[4] *Esaú e Jacob,* chap. xii; *Memorial de Ayres,* "1888—12 de Janeiro."

[5] *Esaú e Jacob,* chap. xii.

[6] *Ibid.,* chaps. xii, xxxii, xl, xlviii–xlix, cxvi.

[7] *Memorial de Ayres,* "1889 [May–June]—Quinta Feira."

[8] Cf. *Deuses de Casaca,* Scene III (THEATRO).

[9] E.g., *Esaú e Jacob,* chap. xl.

[10] *Memorial de Ayres,* "1888—Fim de Maio."

[11] See, for example, *Memorial de Ayres,* "1889—8 de Abril" and "15 de Maio."

[12] *Ibid.,* "1889—8 de Abril."

[13] *Esaú e Jacob,* chap. xiv.

[14] *Ibid.,* chap. xix.

[15] On this point, see Barreto Filho, *Introdução a Machado de Assis* (Rio, A.G.I.R., 1947), pp. 24–27.

[16] As seen, for example, in his criticism of the Church (chap. 9, this study). Cf. Lúcia Miguel Pereira, *História da Literatura Brasileira XII: Prosa de Ficção de 1870 a 1920* (Rio, Olympio, 1950), pp. 94–95.

[17] For an introduction to Machado de Assis's writings on politics, one may consult R. Magalhães Junior, *Machado de Assis Desconhecido* (Rio, Civilização Brasileira, 1955).

[18] E.g., "Valério," "Um Almôço," "O Empréstimo," "Fôlha Rôta," "Pai Contra Mãe."

[19] See, for example, his columns on José de Alencar and on Joaquim Manuel de Macedo, "Semana Literária," *Diário do Rio de Janeiro,* March 6 and 13, May 1 and 8, 1866 (CRITICA THEATRAL); letter of Jan. 29, 1868, to José de Alencar, published in *O Correio Mercantil* (Rio), March 1, 1868 (CORRESPONDENCIA).

[20] This concern was enunciated early, e.g., the poem "Minha Musa," published in 1856 (POESIA E PROSA). Cf. in the same volume "Hino Patriótico" (pp. 45–48), and the brief passages of prose on pp. 152, 177, 179, 180, 181, for his continued concern with his native land and its relation to its writers. See also Magalhães Junior, *Machado de Assis Desconhecido,* pp. 43, 191, 242, and passim.

[21] "Notícia da Atual Literatura Brasileira—Instinto de Nacionalidade," *O Novo Mundo* (New York), March 24, 1873 (CRITICA LITTERARIA); "Comentários da Semana," *Diário do Rio de Janeiro,* March 24, 1862 (CHRONICAS, I); speech before the Academia Brasileira de Letras, Dec. 7, 1897 (PAGINAS RECOLHIDAS); letters to Nabuco, June 28, and Aug. 1, 1908 (CORRESPONDENCIA); "Semana Literária," Diário do Rio de Janeiro, March 20, 1866, republished in *Revista do Livro* (Rio), Sept., 1958, p. 188. Cf. Barreto Filho, *Introdução a Machado de Assis,* pp. 32–33.

[22] For Machado de Assis's intense feeling on this point, see *Esaú e*

Jacob (chap. xliii), where the proud father Santos wants to publish his son's speech in Rio de Janeiro and the provinces, and have it translated into French ("In French it will most likely be even better"); and his column "A Semana," *Gazeta de Notícias* (Rio), March 5, 1893, July 21, 1895, and Dec. 15, 1895 (A SEMANA, I, II, III). Cf. José Veríssimo, *Estudos de Literatura Brasileira: Primeira Série,* pp. 253–259; and Magalhães Junior, *Machado de Assis Desconhecido,* pp. 114–115, 153.

[23] E.g., Arturo Torres Ríoseco, *Expressão Literária do Novo Mundo,* trans. Valdemar Cavalcanti (Rio, C.E.B., 1945), p. 348; Astrojildo Pereira, "Machado de Assis: Romancista do Segundo Reinado," *Revista do Brasil,* June, 1939, as quoted by Francisco de Assis Barbosa in *Manual Bibliográfico de Estudos Brasileiros,* ed. Rubens Borba de Moraes and William Berrien (Rio, Gráfica Editora Souza, 1949), p. 687; Lúcia Miguel Pereira, *Prosa de Ficção,* pp. 50, 55–56.

[24] See in particular his "Instinto de Nacionalidade" (CRITICA LITTERARIA); also his column "A Semana," *Gazeta de Notícias,* Aug. 20, 1893 (A SEMANA, I). Cf. p. 173 of the collection POESIA E PROSA: ". . . tudo isso veio na caravela de Colombo."

[25] "Garrett," *Gazeta de Notícias,* Feb. 4, 1899 (CRITICA LITTERARIA).

[26] "Instinto de Nacionalidade" (CRITICA LITTERARIA).

[27] "Guilherme Malta—Carta ao Sr. Conselheiro Lopes Neto," *Jornal do Comércio* (Rio), July 2, 1872 (CRITICA LITTERARIA, under the title "'Un Cuento Endemoniado' e 'La Mujer Misteriosa'").

[28] "A Semana," *Gazeta de Notícias,* July 28, 1895 (A SEMANA, II).

[29] "A Semana," *Gazeta de Notícias,* Dec. 27, 1896 (A SEMANA, III).

For further examples of Machado's belief in "multiple plagiarism," see: "Lyra dos Vinte Anos," *Diário do Rio de Janeiro,* June 26, 1866 (CRITICA LITTERARIA); "História de Quinze Dias—Livro I," *Ilustração Brasileira,* Jan. 1, 1877 (CHRONICAS, III); "Antonio José e Molière," *Revista Brasileira* (Rio), July 15, 1879 (CRITICA THEATRAL [under the title "Antonio José"]); foreword to "O Almada" (POESIAS COMPLETAS). One is also tempted to cite a letter, purported to be from an anonymous contributor, which Machado de Assis published in his column in *O Futuro* (Rio), May 1, 1863 (CHRONICAS, I), for the sentiments are identical with his.

[30] Machado de Assis, *Adelaide Ristori: Folhetins* (Rio, Academia Brasileira de Letras, 1955), pp. 69–70.

[31] "Occidentais '1802–1885'" (POESIAS COMPLETAS).

[32] "A Semana," *Gazeta de Notícias,* April 23, 1893 (A SEMANA, I); cf. "A Semana" for Dec. 30, 1894 (A SEMANA, II).

[33] "A Semana," *Gazeta de Notícias,* April 26, 1893 (A SEMANA, III).